ᴀNCED

Collected Pia

ɴN COATES POPULAR PIANO LIBRARY

Since 1976, Dan Coates has arranged thousands of popular music titles. Composers and artists such as John Williams, Burt Bacharach, and Elton John have expressed total confidence in Dan's ability to create outstanding piano arrangements that retain the essence of the original music. He has arranged everything from movie, television, and Broadway themes to chart-topping pop and rock titles. In addition to creating piano arrangements for players of all levels, Dan also composes original music for student pianists.

Collected here in this book are 47 of Dan's popular arrangements for advanced piano, divided into four sections: Standards, Ballads, Movie Solos, and Broadway Hits. These diverse arrangements are sure to provide accomplished pianists and their audiences with hours of entertainment.

Produced by
Alfred Music
P.O. Box 10003
Van Nuys, CA 91410-0003
alfred.com

Printed in USA.

ISBN-10: 0-7390-9862-4
ISBN-13: 978-0-7390-9862-2

Contents

At Last

Music by Harry Warren
Lyrics by Mack Gordon
Arranged by Dan Coates

9

11

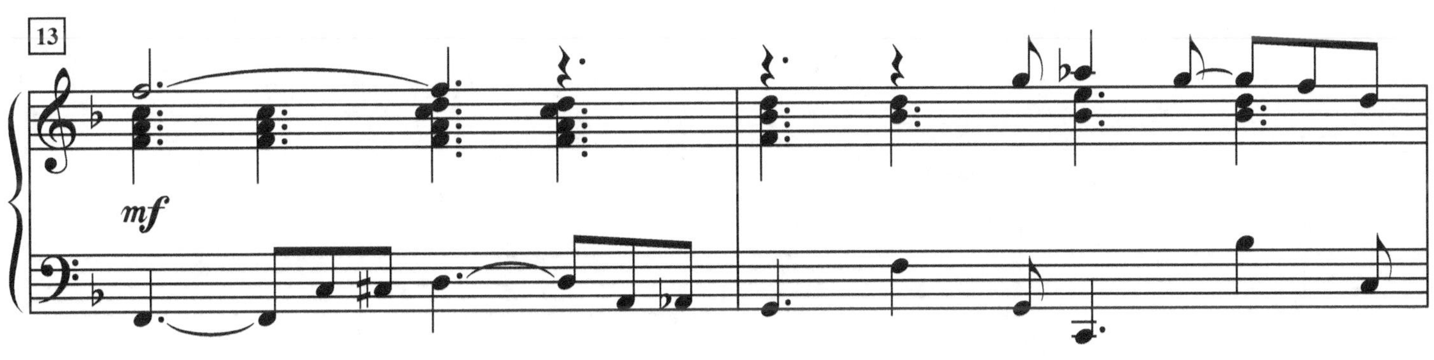
13
mf

15

17
3

19
5
3
1
1
2-1
1
2
1
5

21
mp
1
1

23
4
2
1
2
3
4
2

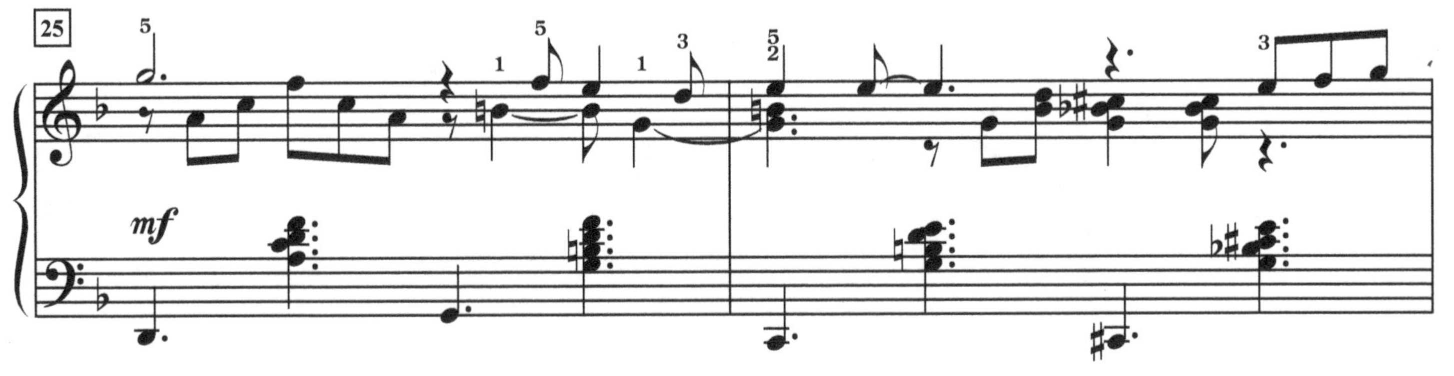
25
mf

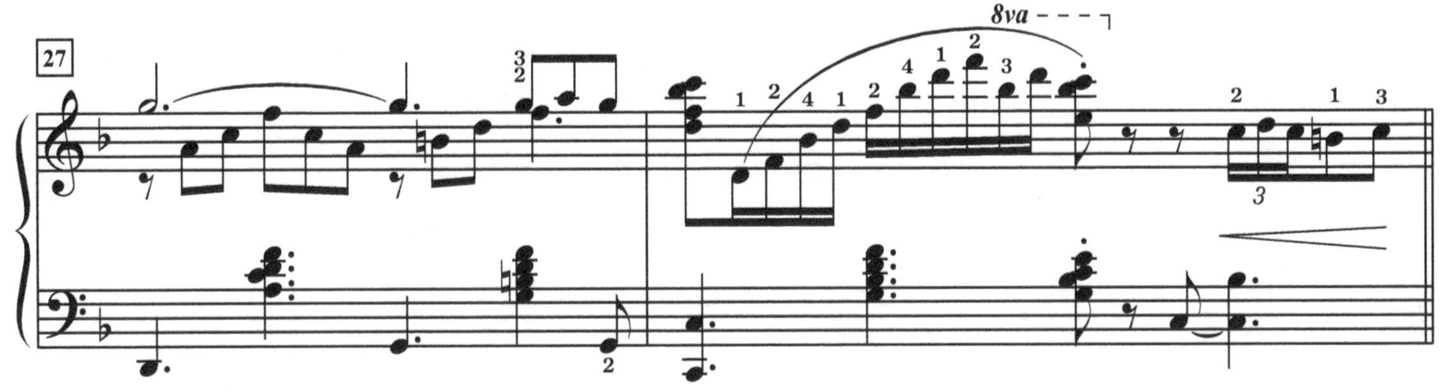
27
8va

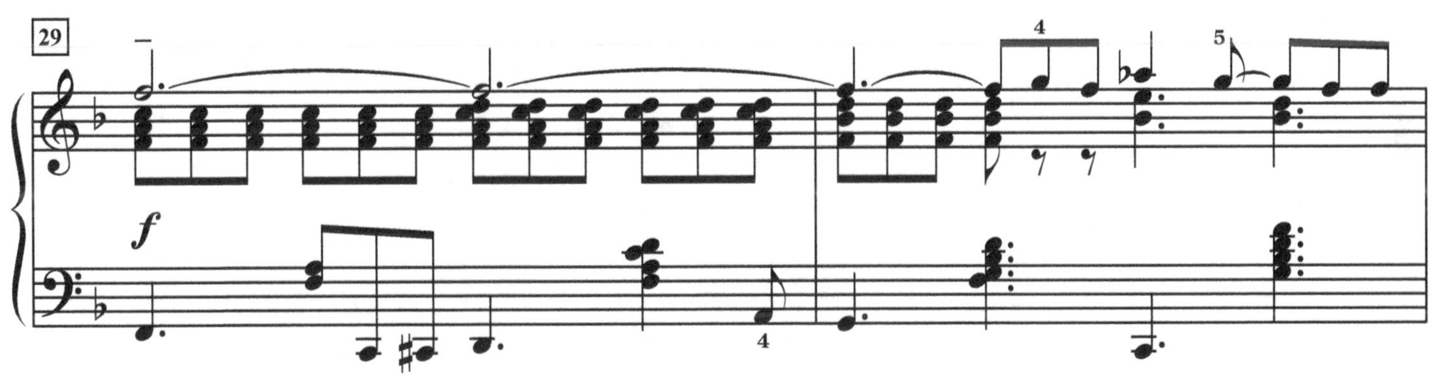
29
f

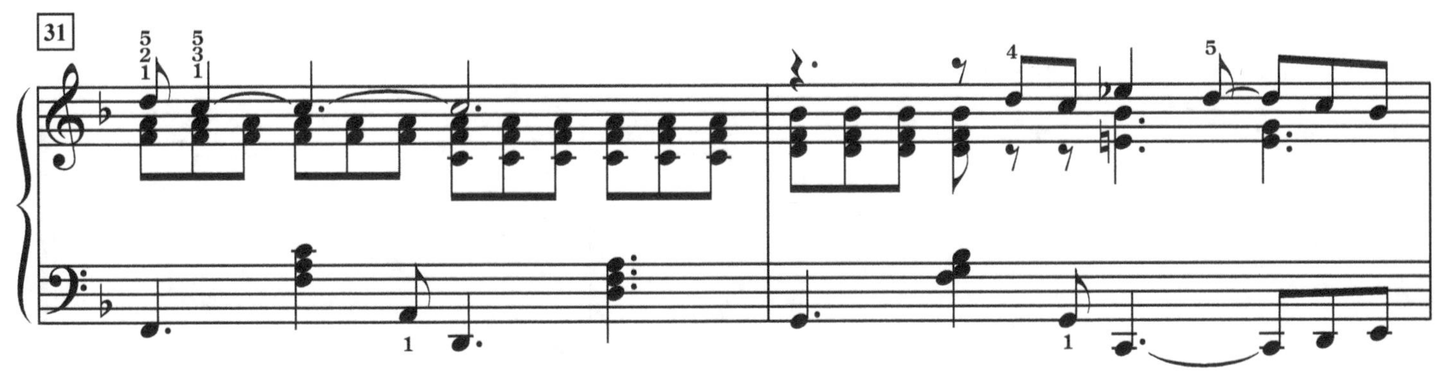
31

33
1.
mf

35

37
2.
a tempo
mf
rit.

39
8va
mp
rit.
p

Bewitched, Bothered and Bewildered

Words by Lorenz Hart
Music by Richard Rodgers
Arranged by Dan Coates

13
5
2
1
3
3
2
1
5
4
2
1
2

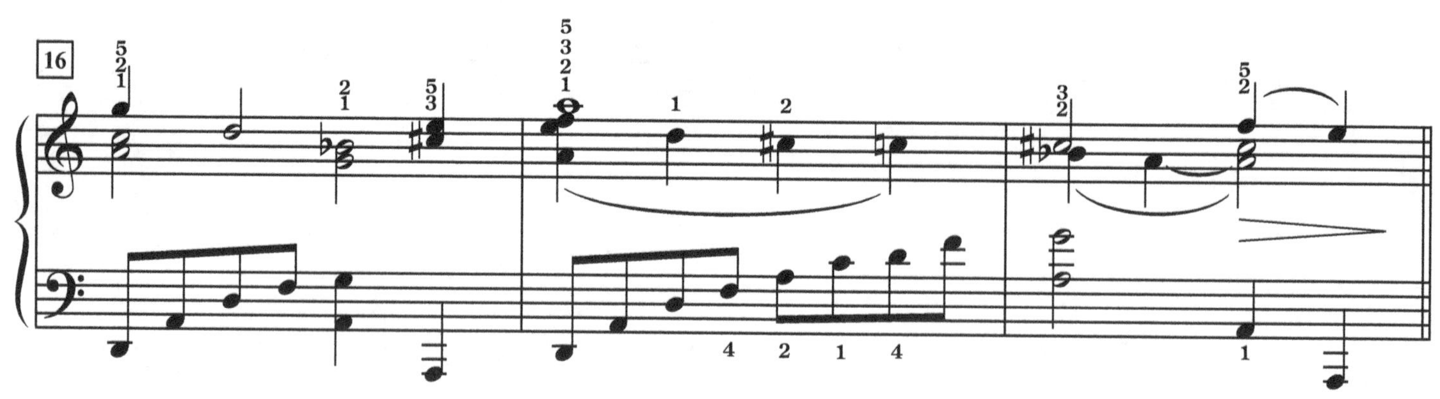
16
5
2
1
2
1
5
3
5
3
2
1
1
2
3
2
5
2
4
2
1
4
1

19
5
2
1
mp
più mosso
5

22
2
1
1
2
3
5
1
2
3
mf
4
2
1
2

a tempo
25
f
rit.
mf

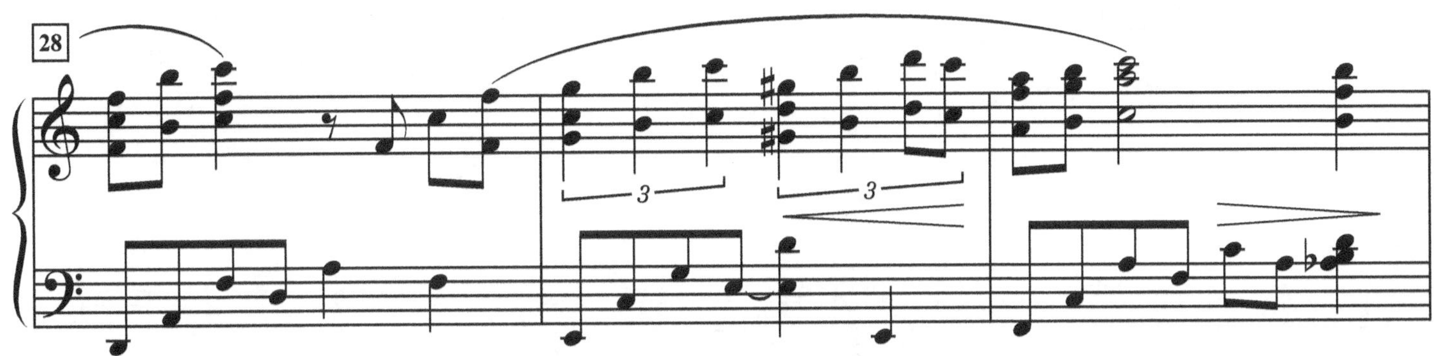
28

31
1.

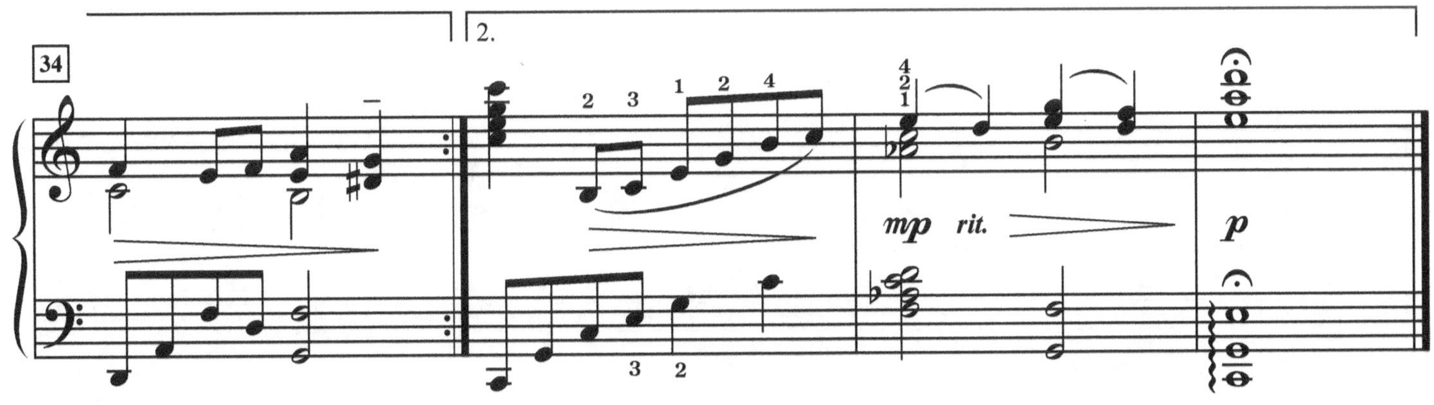
34
2.
mp rit.
p

Blue Moon

Music by Richard Rodgers
Lyrics by Lorenz Hart
Arranged by Dan Coates

9
3
11
2
1
2
4
1
1
13
mf
15
17
5
3
2
3
4

19
mp
3
3
21
4
mf
4
4
23
25
2
5
3
2
3
4
27
5
4
2
5
3
cresc.
5
4
2
1
2
4
1
1
1
1
3
5
3
1
3
2

29
f
31
mf
33
35
1.
mp
37
2.
mp
rit.
p

Fascinating Rhythm

Music and Lyrics by
George Gershwin and Ira Gershwin
Arranged by Dan Coates

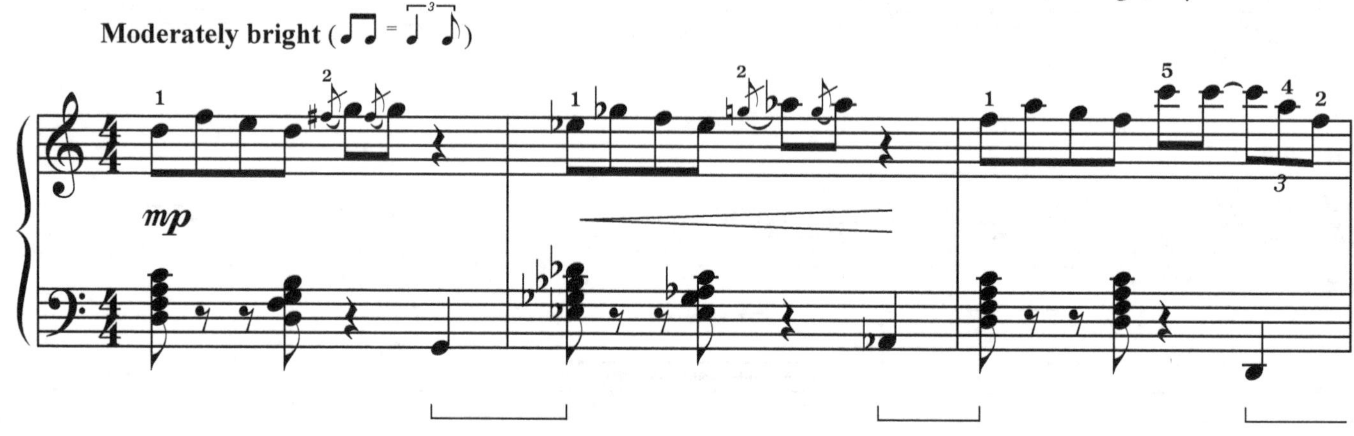

10

13
mf

16
f

19
mf

22

25

28
f

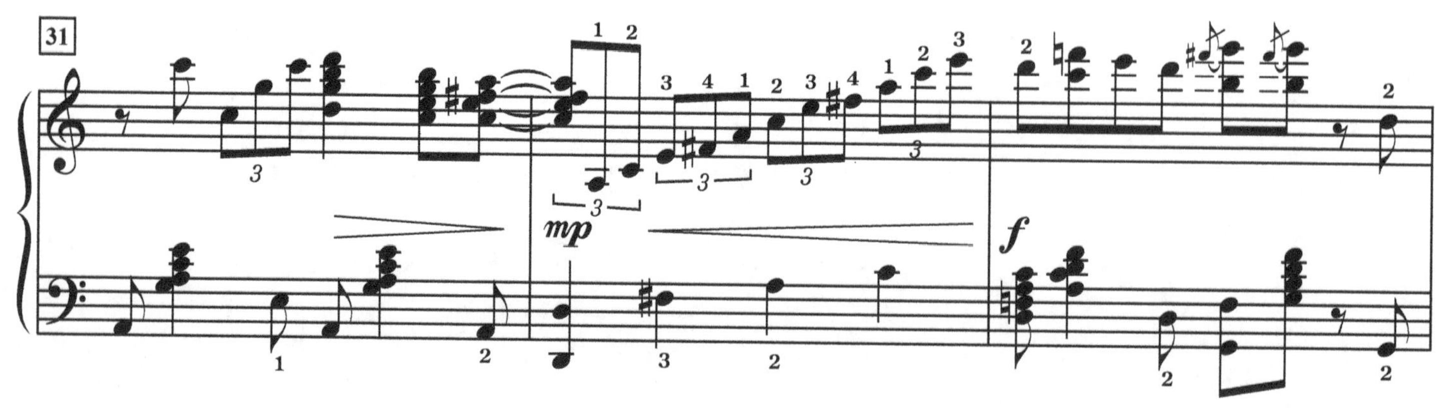
31
mp
f

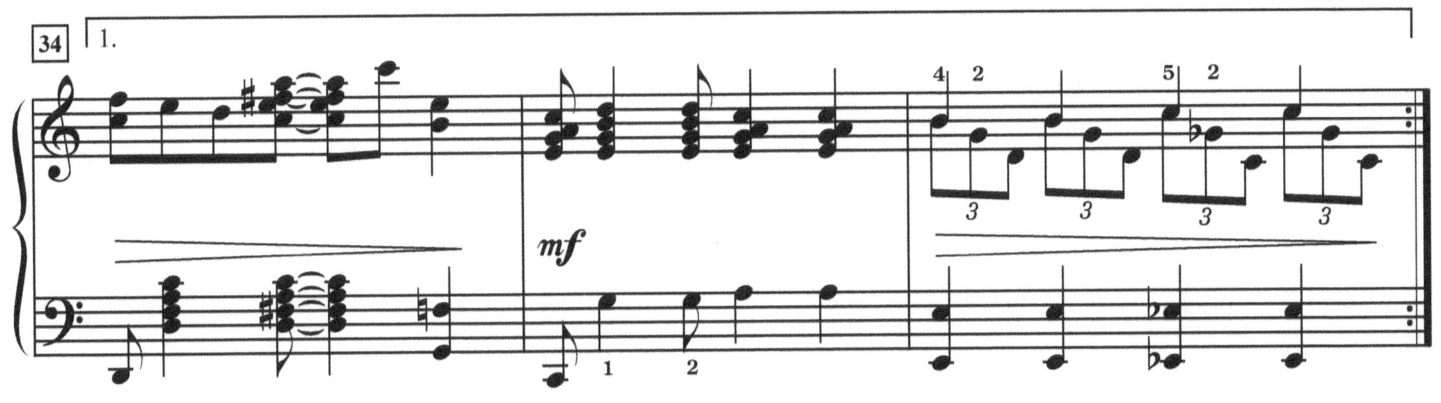
34
1.
4 2
5 2
3
3
3
3
mf
1
2

37
2.
3
2
1
2
2
3

8va
40
ff
2
2
1

42
5
3
2
3
3
3
5
2
1
5
3
2
1
f
3
1
2
8va

How High the Moon

Lyrics by Nancy Hamilton
Music by Morgan Lewis
Arranged by Dan Coates

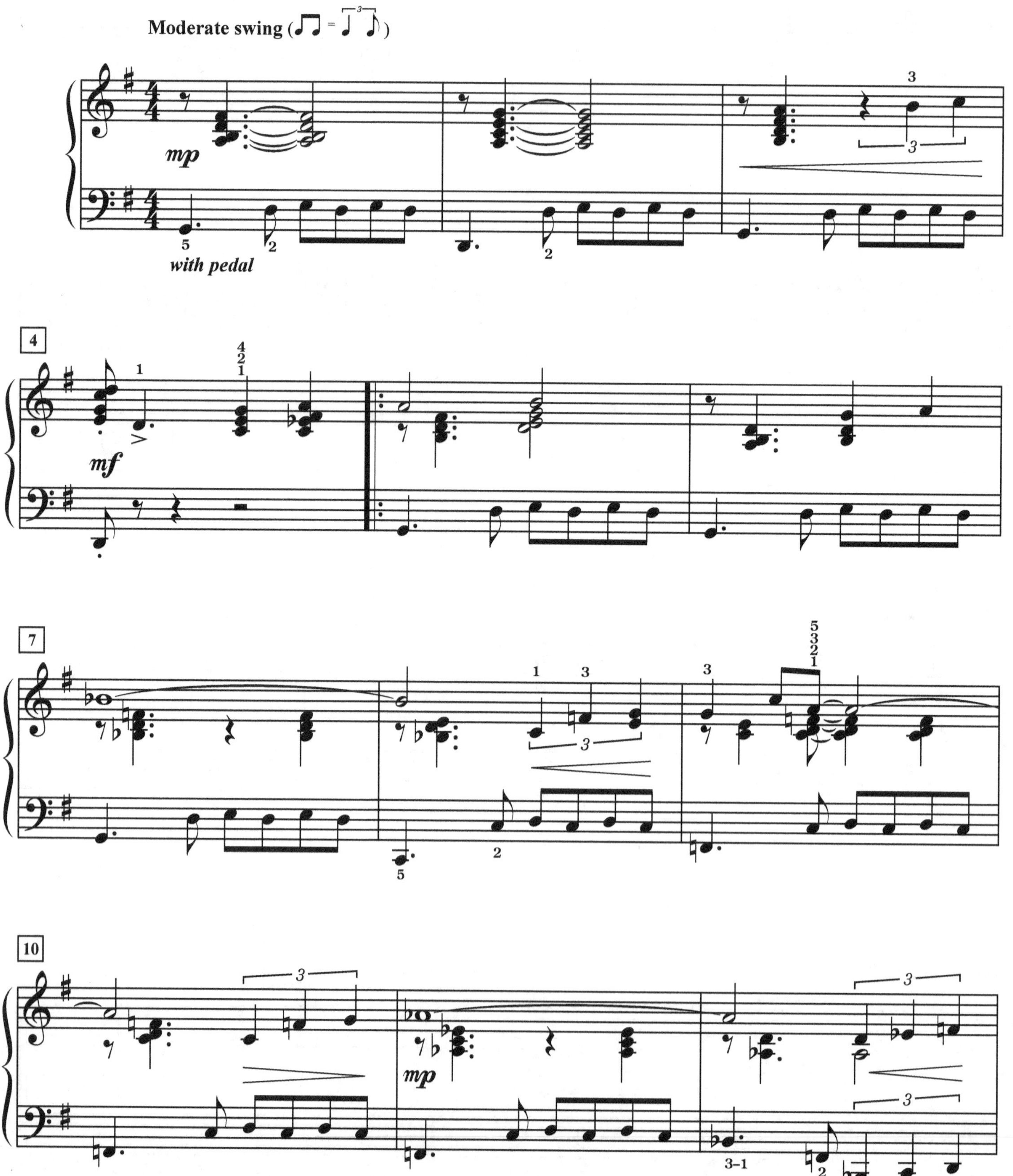

13
16
cresc.
19
f
mf
22
25

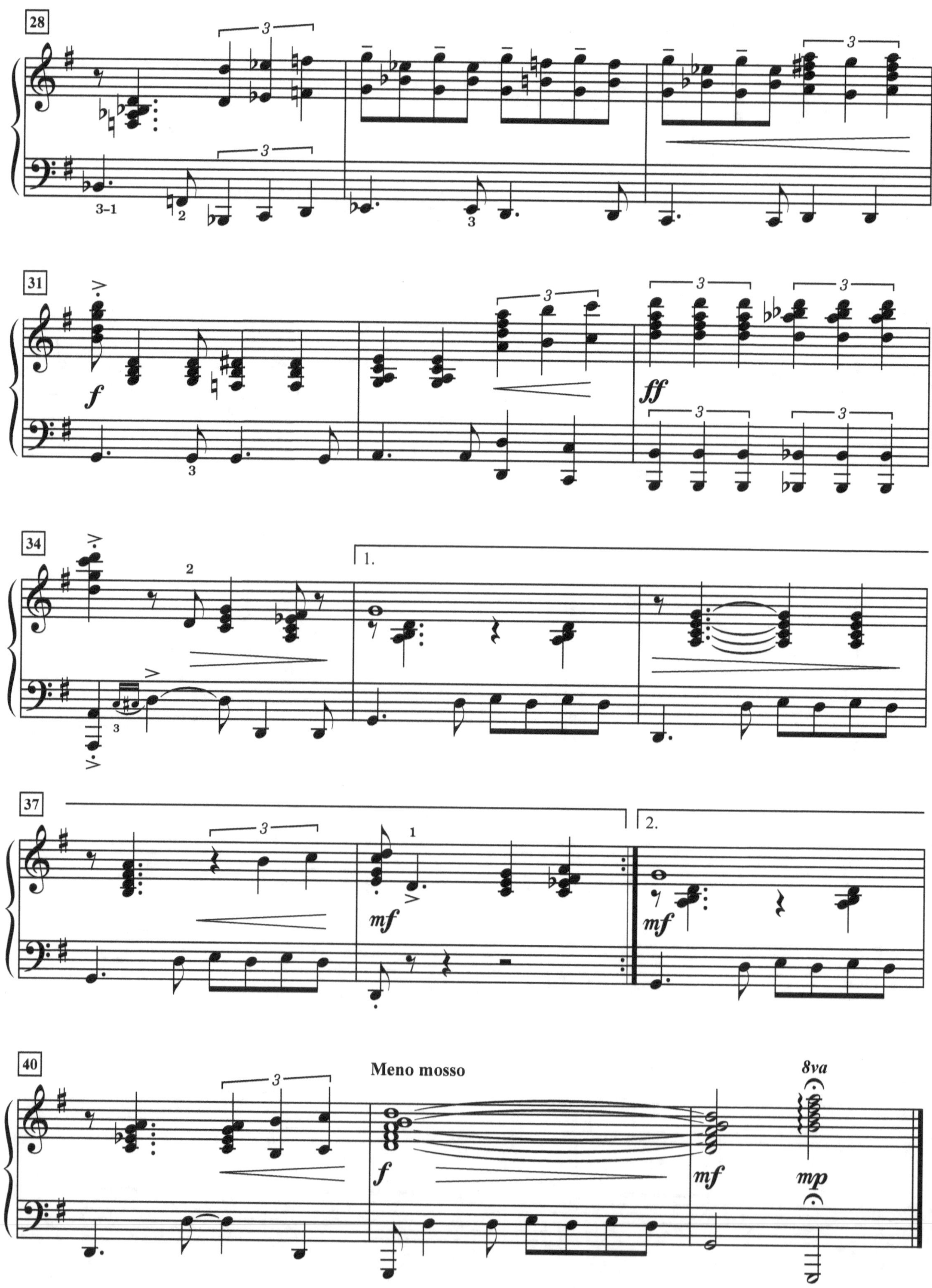
28
31
34
1.
37
2.
40
Meno mosso
8va

I'll Be Seeing You

Music by Sammy Fain
Lyrics by Irving Kahal
Arranged by Dan Coates

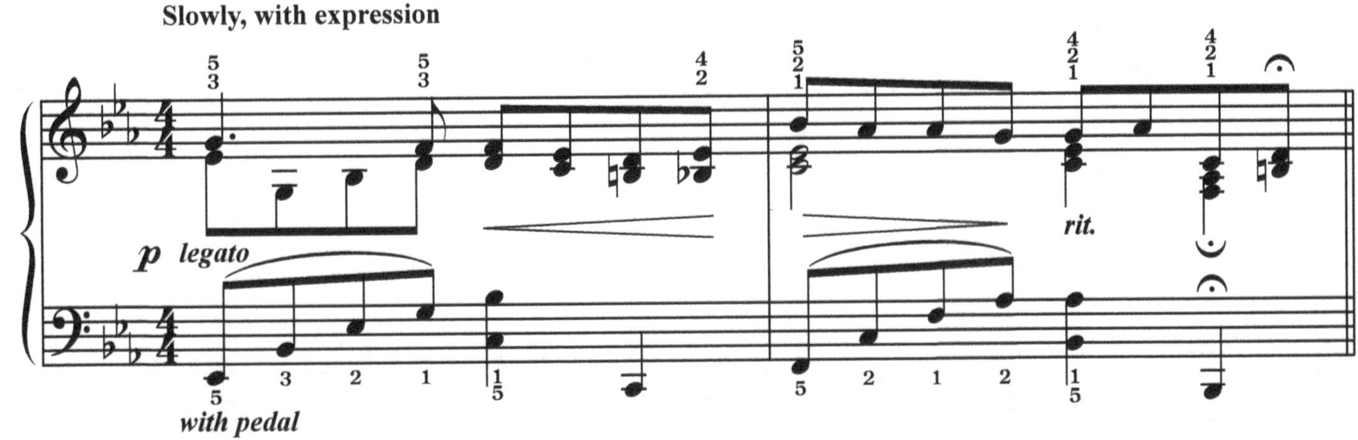

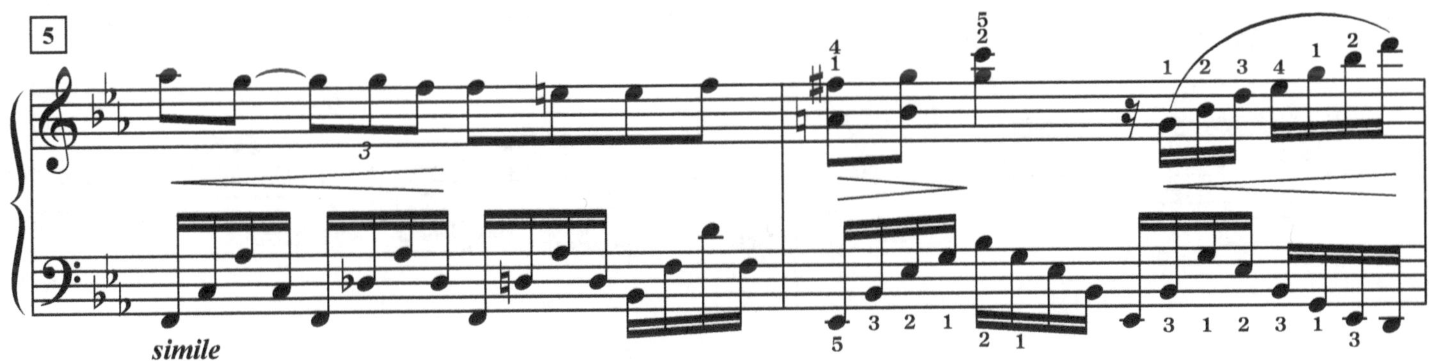

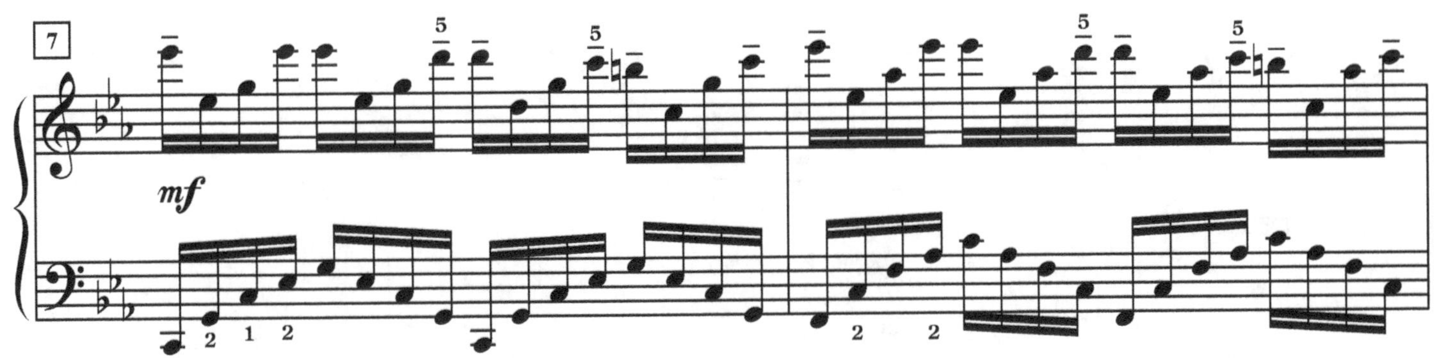

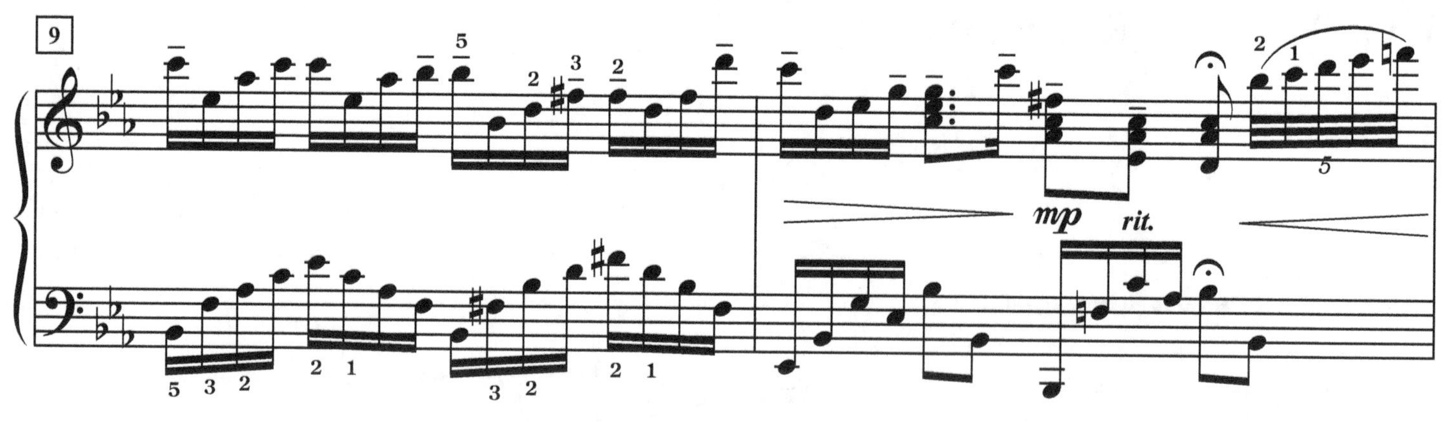
9
mp
rit.

a tempo
8va
11
mf

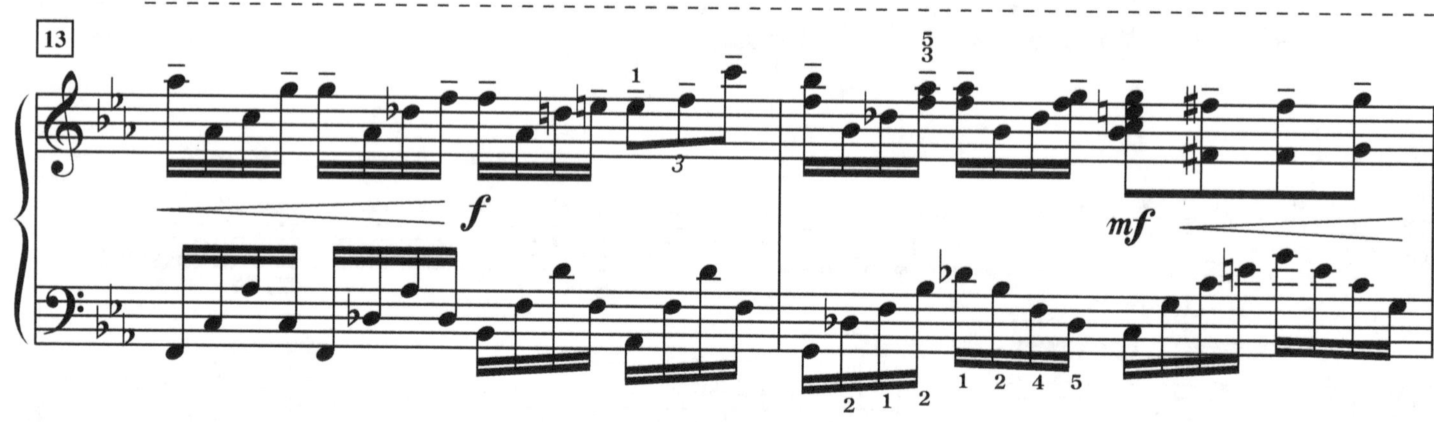
13
f
mf

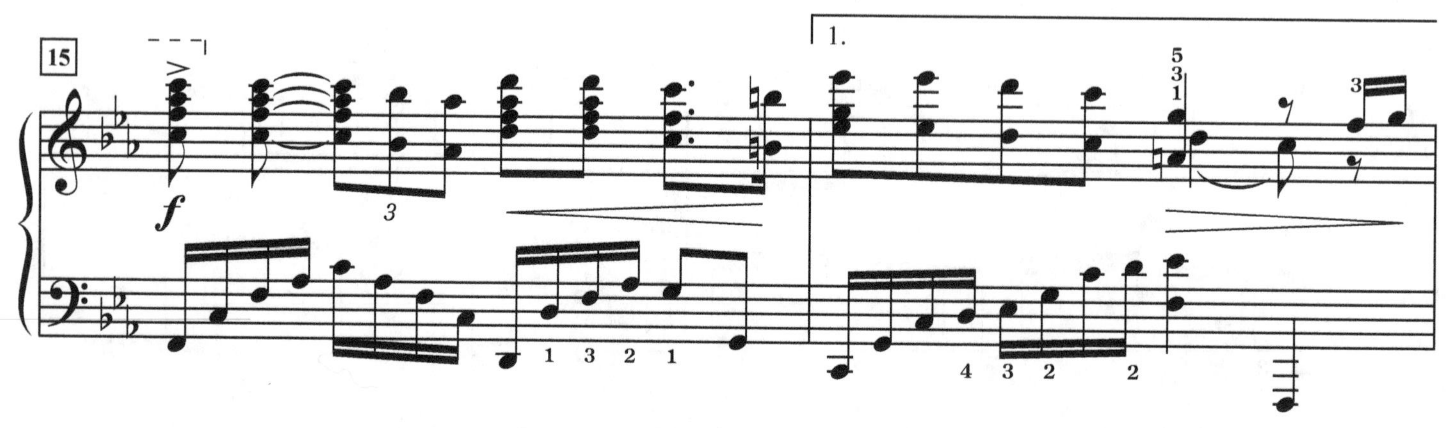
15
f
1.

17
mf
mp

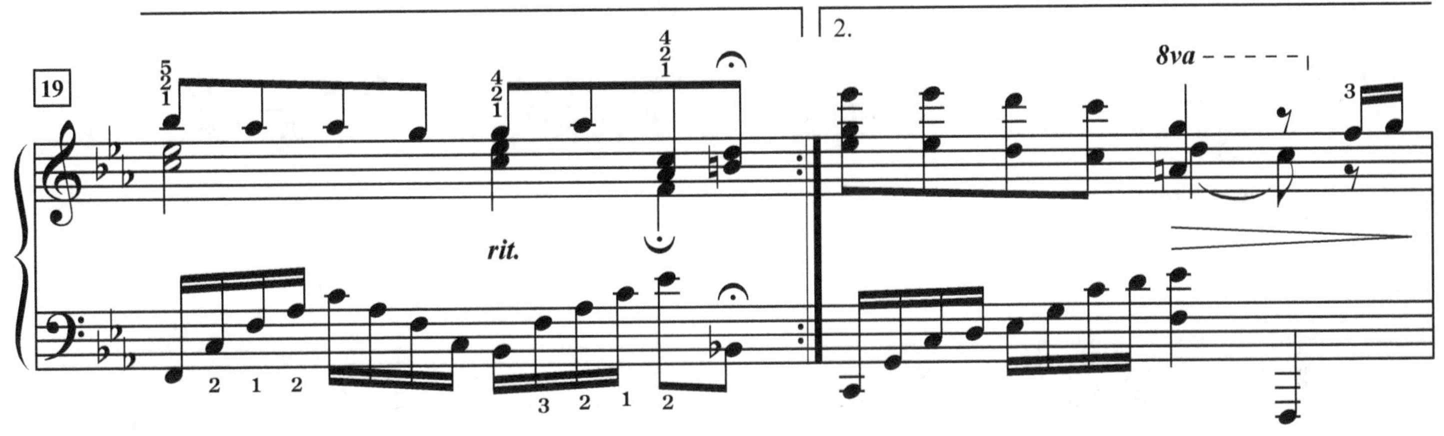
19
rit.
2.
8va

21
a tempo
mf
rit.
mp

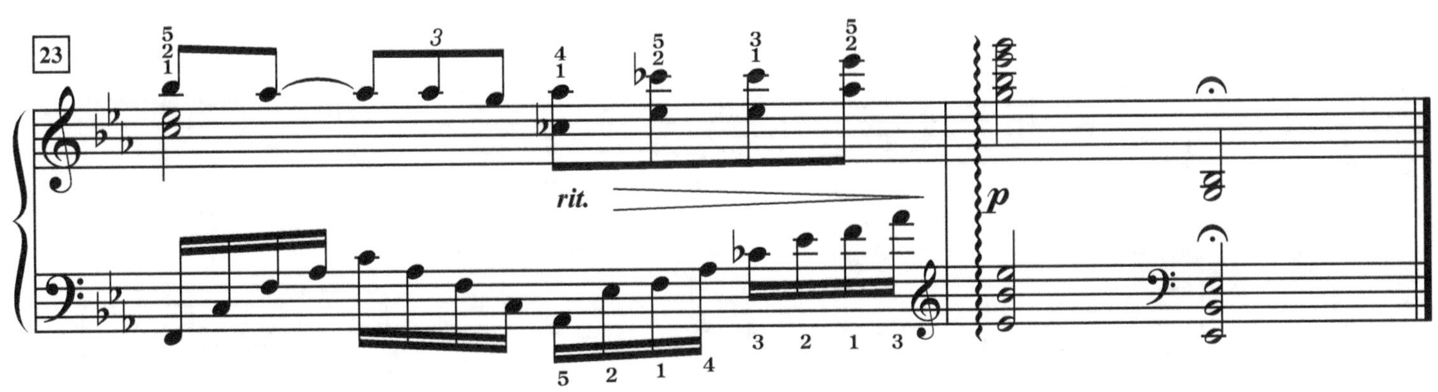
23
rit.
p

Mountain Greenery

Words by Lorenz Hart
Music by Richard Rodgers
Arranged by Dan Coates

swing
13
3
2
1
5
f
5

16
2

19
5
mf
2

22

25
1
5
1
5
4
2
1
2
3
3
2
1
5
4
1

even eighths
swing
28
f

31
1

1.
34
1
1
3
5
3

37
2.
mf

40
ff

43
f dim.

46
even eighths
swing
mp
f
mf
8va

My Foolish Heart

Words by Ned Washington
Music by Victor Young
Arranged by Dan Coates

13
mf
16
19
mp
22
25
mf

28
f
mf
31
34
1.
8va
mp
37
39
2.
mp
rit.
p
pp

Till

Music by Charles Danvers
Arranged by Dan Coates

13

16

19

f

25
mf
mp

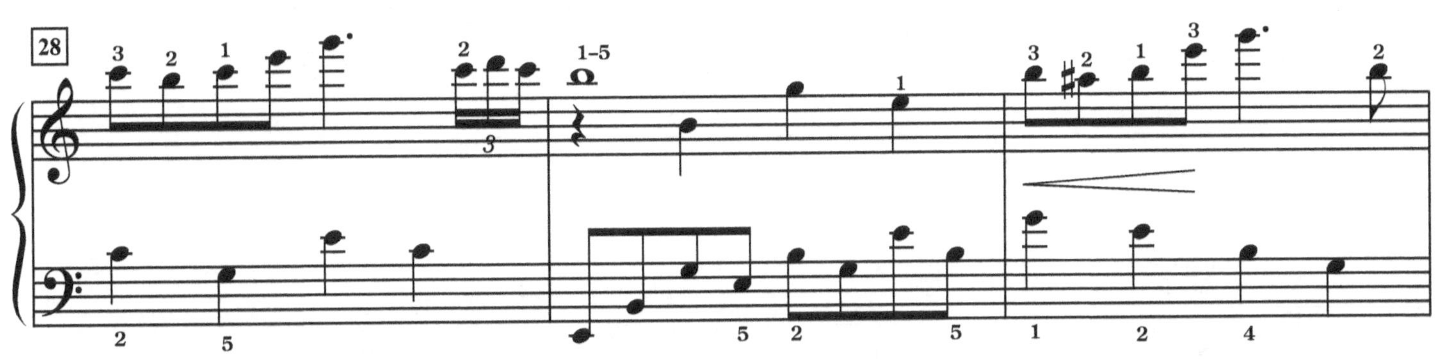
28

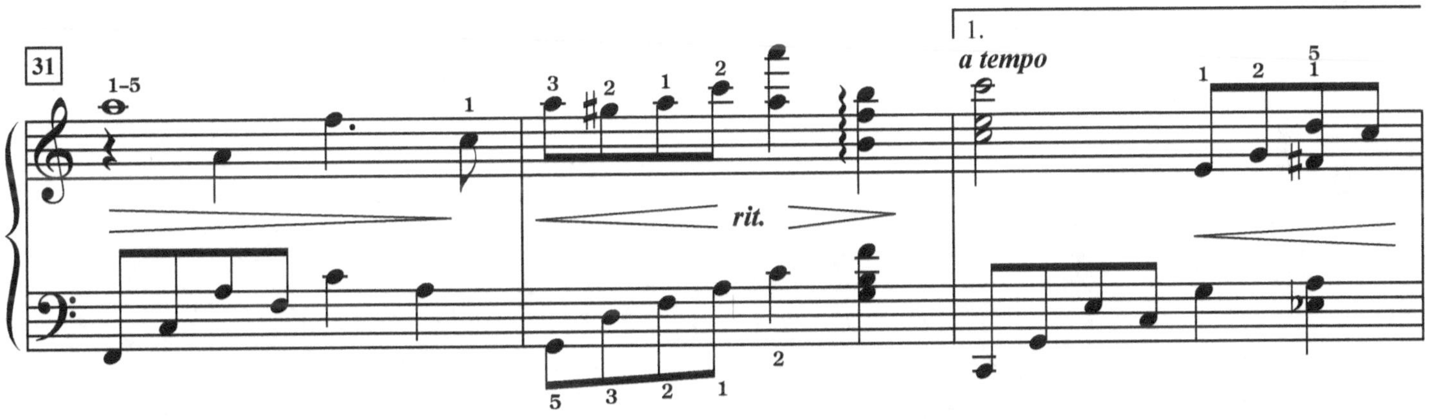
31
rit.
1.
a tempo

34
2.
8va
rit.
p
pp
8va

Night and Day

Words and Music by Cole Porter
Arranged by Dan Coates

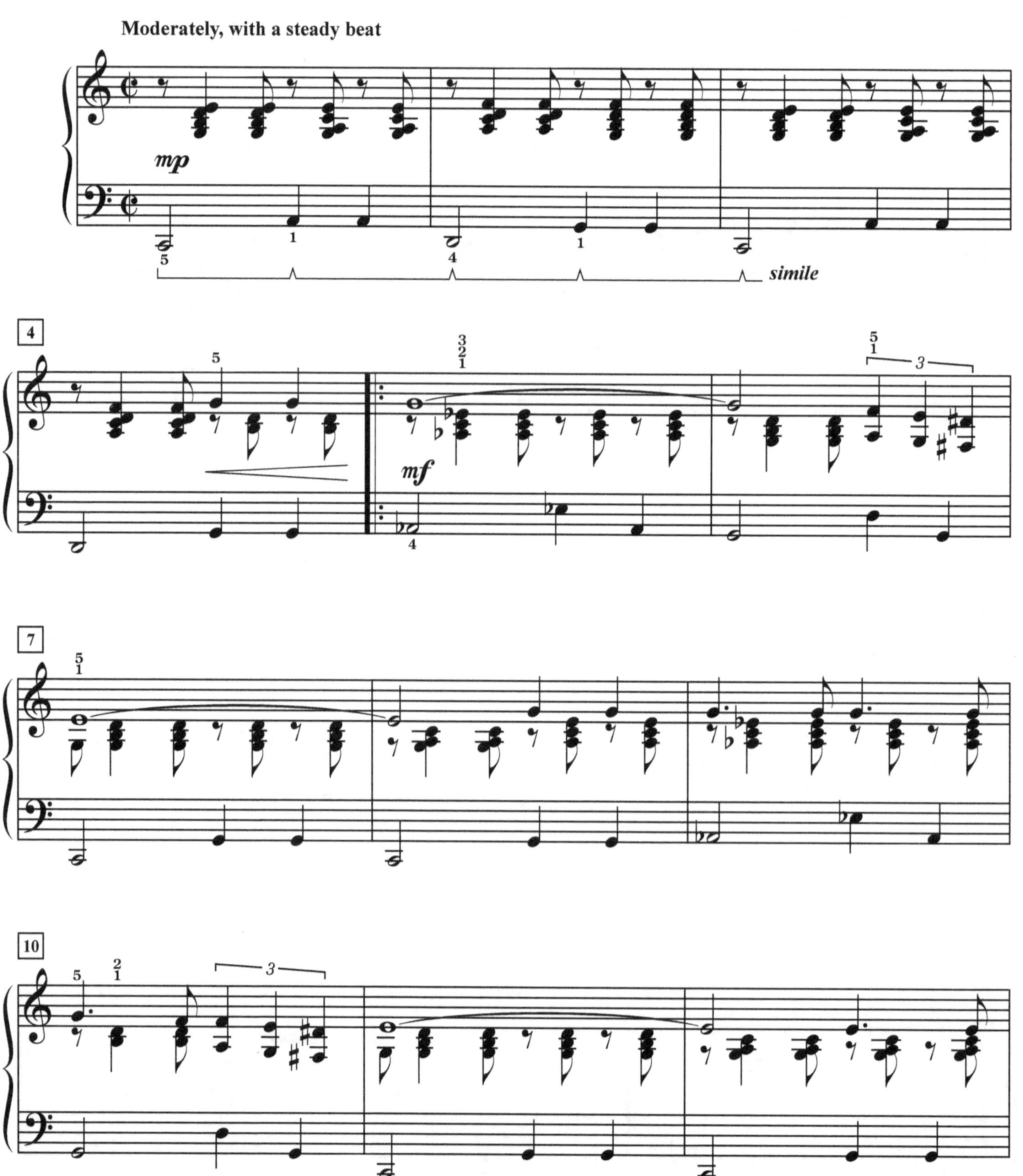

13
16
19
22
25
mf

28
31
34
mp
37
40

43
3
3
mf
46
3
3
f
49
1.
rit.
52
2.
mf
55
8va
mp
8va

Weekend in New England

Words and Music by Randy Edelman
Arranged by Dan Coates

17
rit.

21
a tempo
mf

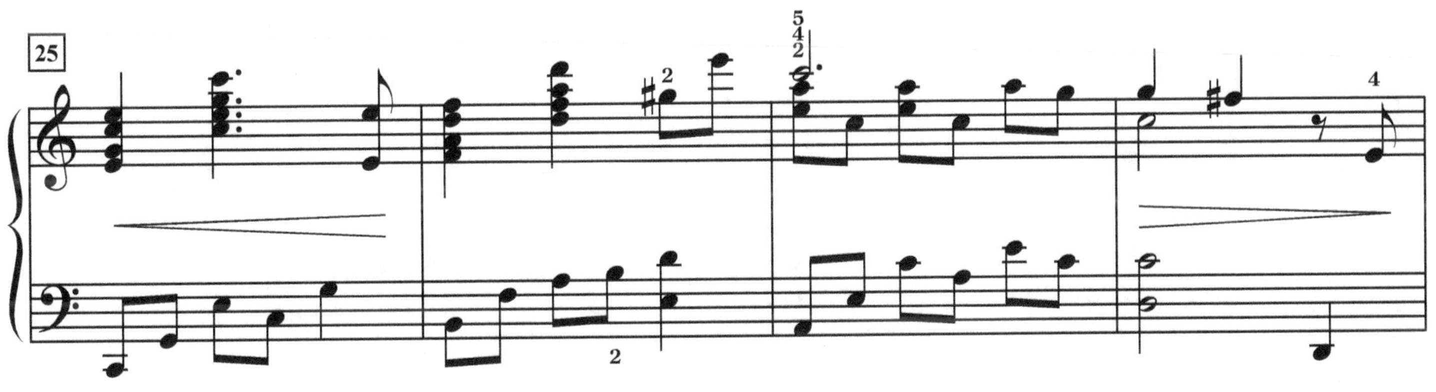
25

29
1.
mp

33
2.

37
f

41
mf

45

49
cresc. poco a poco
5
2
5

8va
53
2
5
1
4

56
f
5
2

59

62
ff
f

65
8va
dim.

68
mp

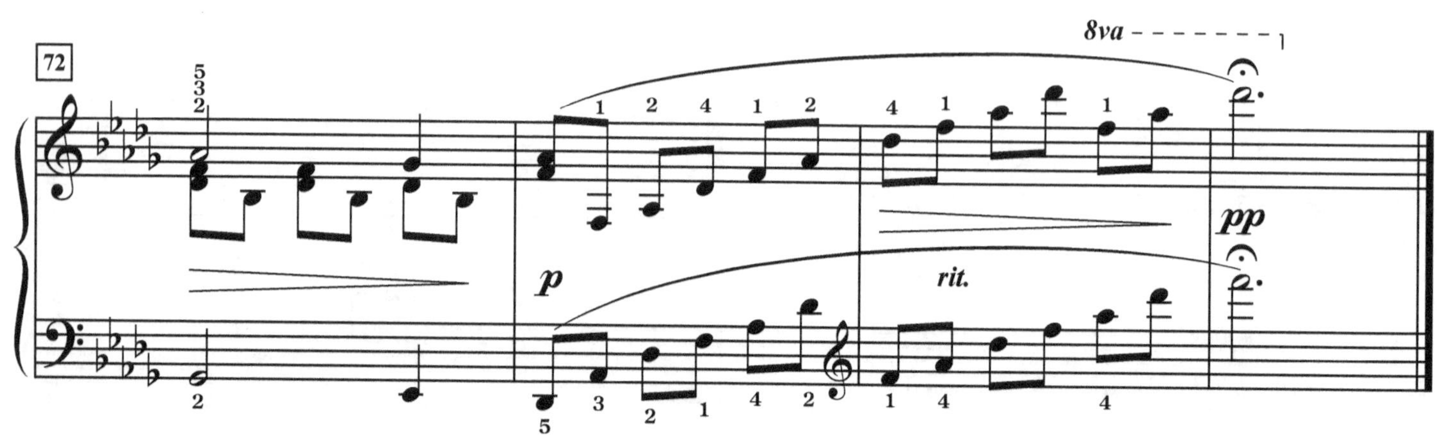
72
8va
p
rit.
pp

Where Do You Start

Lyrics by Alan and Marilyn Bergman
Music by Johnny Mandel
Arranged by Dan Coates

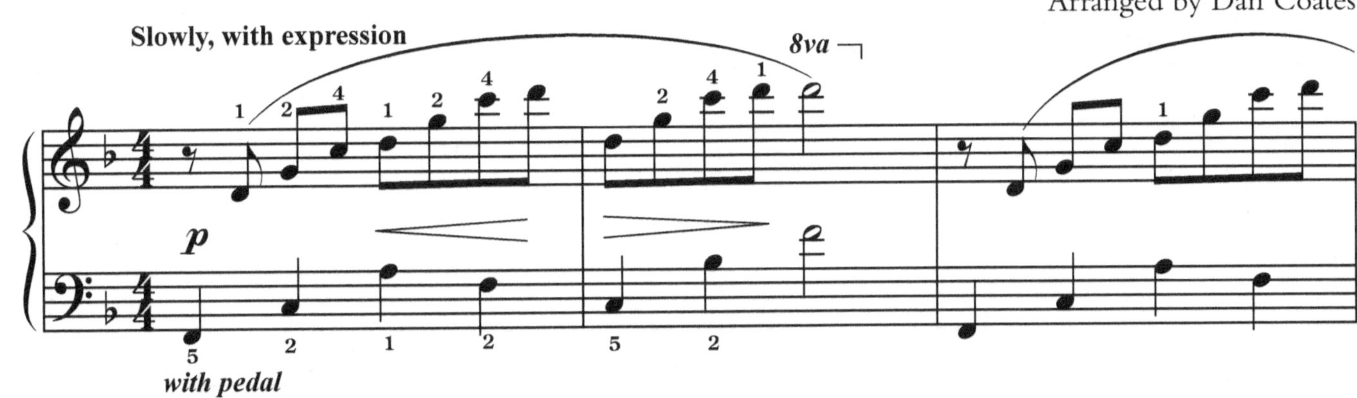

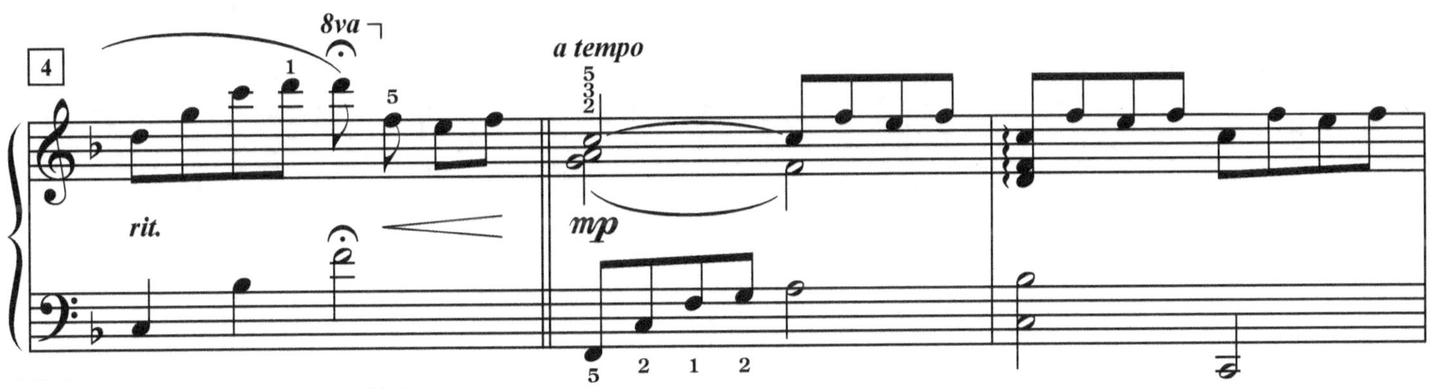

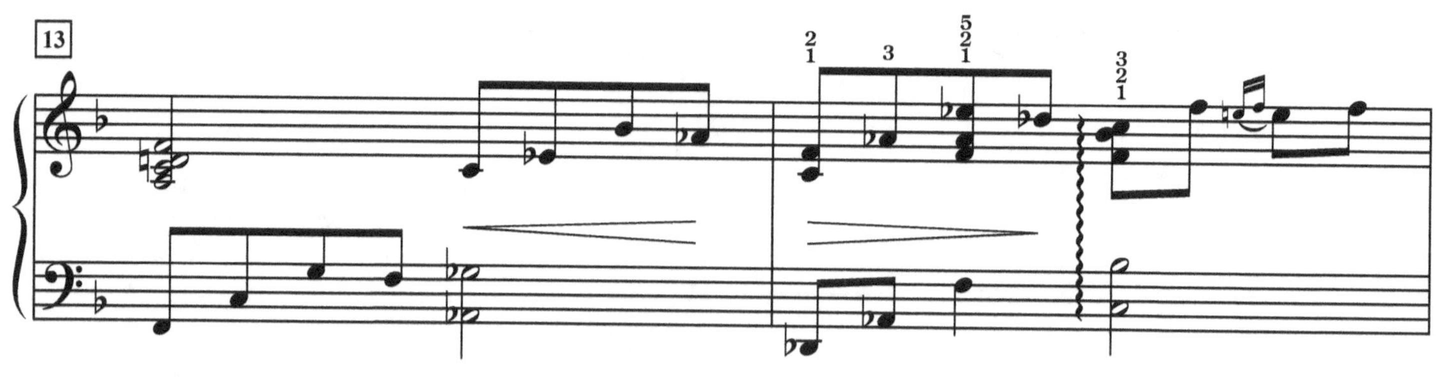
13
2
1
3
5
2
1
3
2
1

15

18
2
1
4
mf

21
5
2
3
5
1
2
3
mp

8va
rit.

a tempo
mf

33
mp

36
mf
2
4
2

38
f
5

40
4
2
5

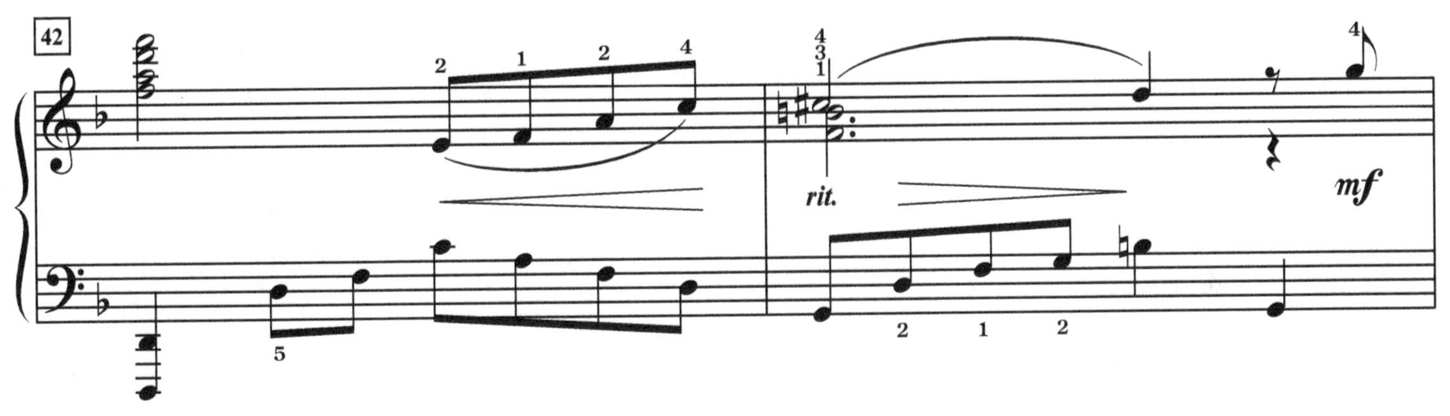
42
rit.
mf

a tempo
44
molto rit.

a tempo
46
8va
mp

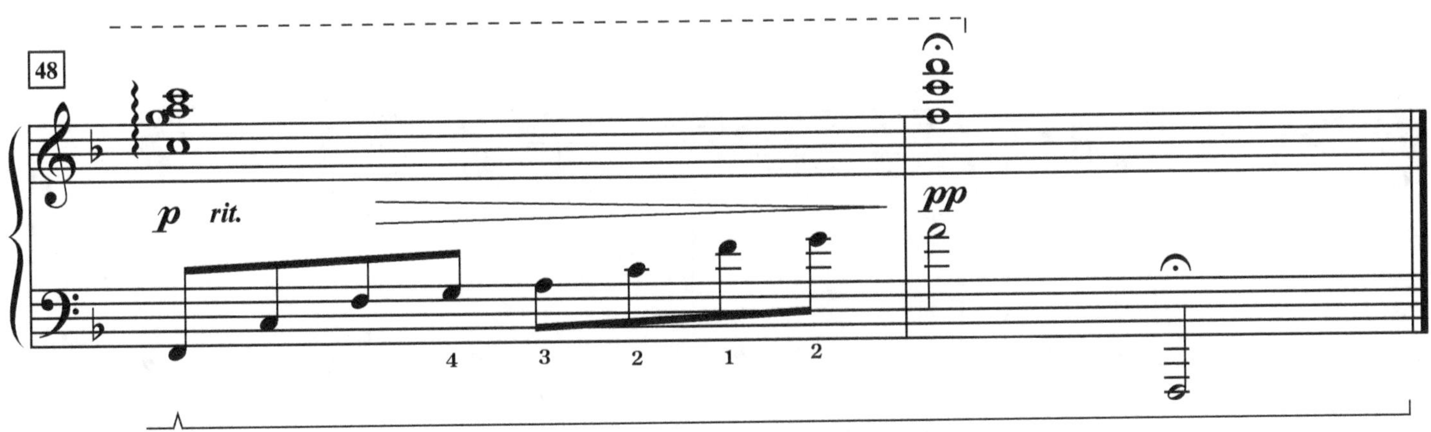
48
p rit.
pp

At This Moment
(from *Family Ties*)

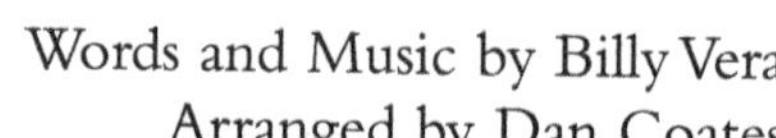

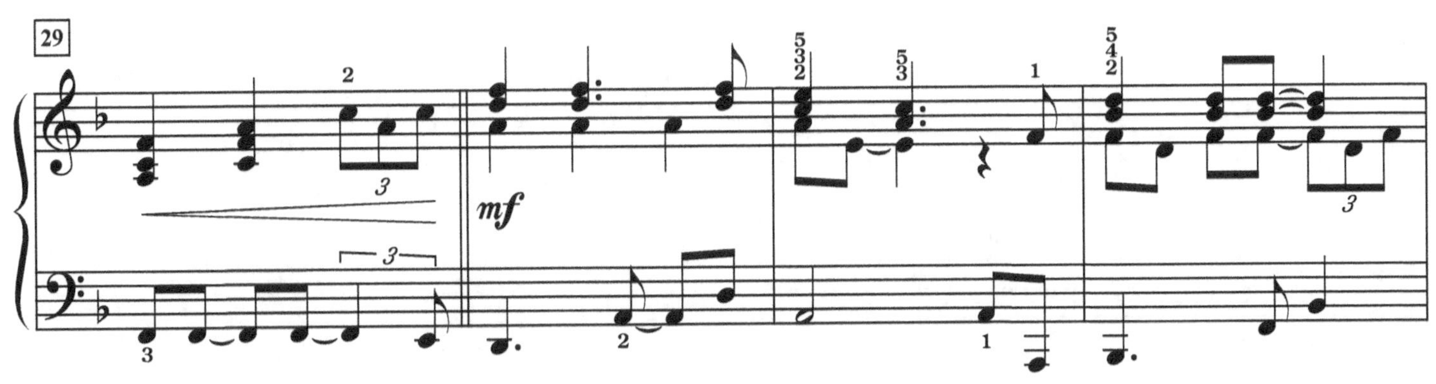

Ballads

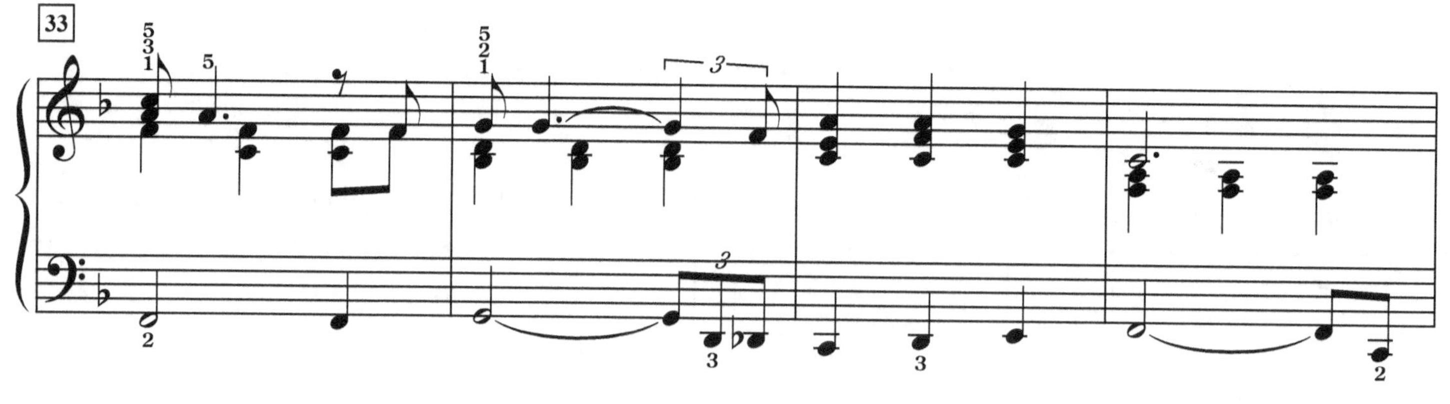
33

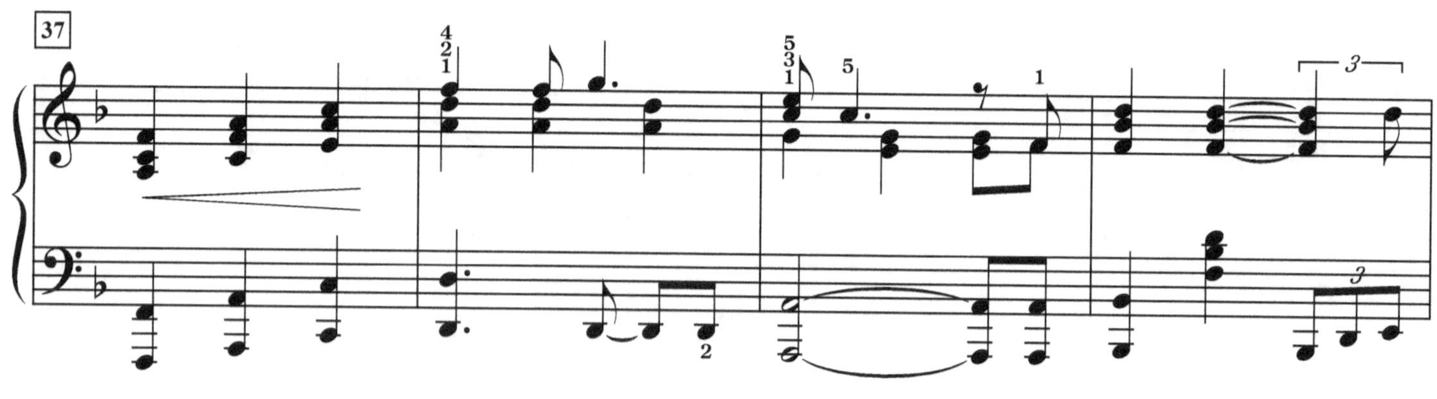
37

41

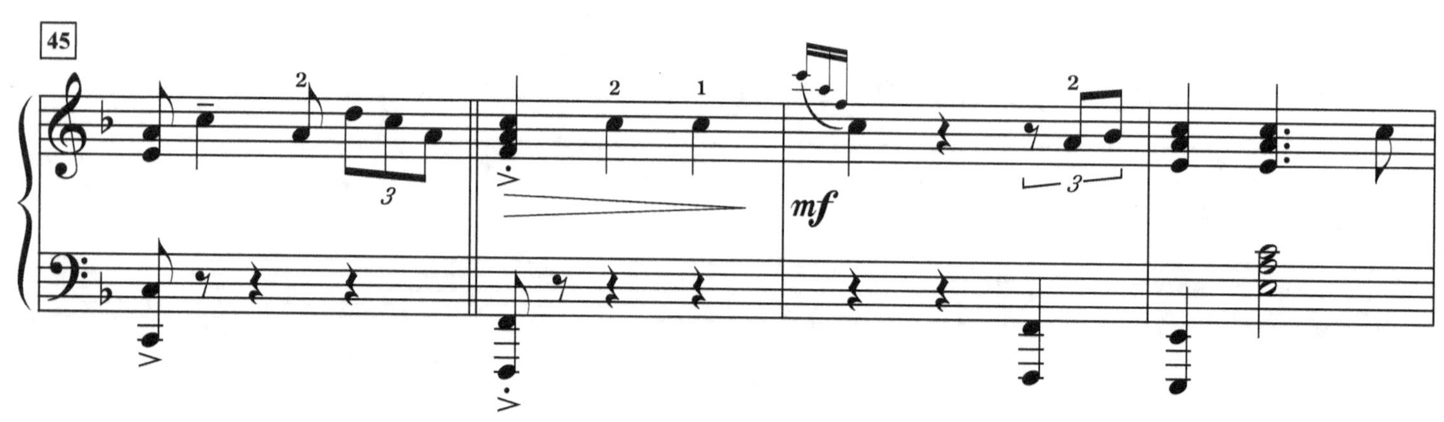
45

49
5
3
1
3
4
3
3
1

53
5
1
3
1
1 3
3
3
1

57
5
3
2 1
1
4
2
f
2

61
3
3

65
ff
f
69
73
a tempo
mf molto rit.
f
77
81
mp
rit.
p

WHAT A WONDERFUL WORLD

Words and Music by
George David Weiss and Bob Thiele
Arranged by Dan Coates

7
mf
3

9
f

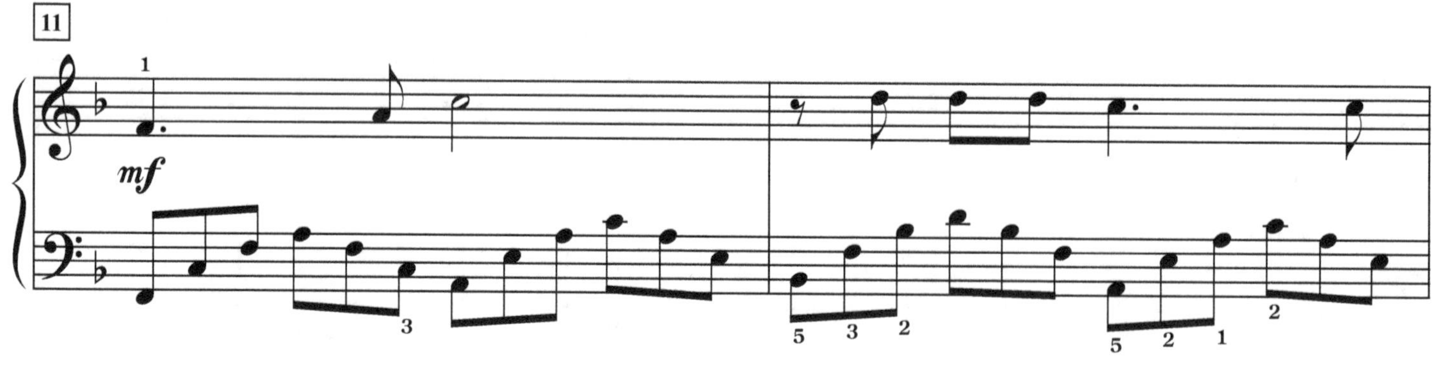
11
mf

13

15

17

19

21

23
f

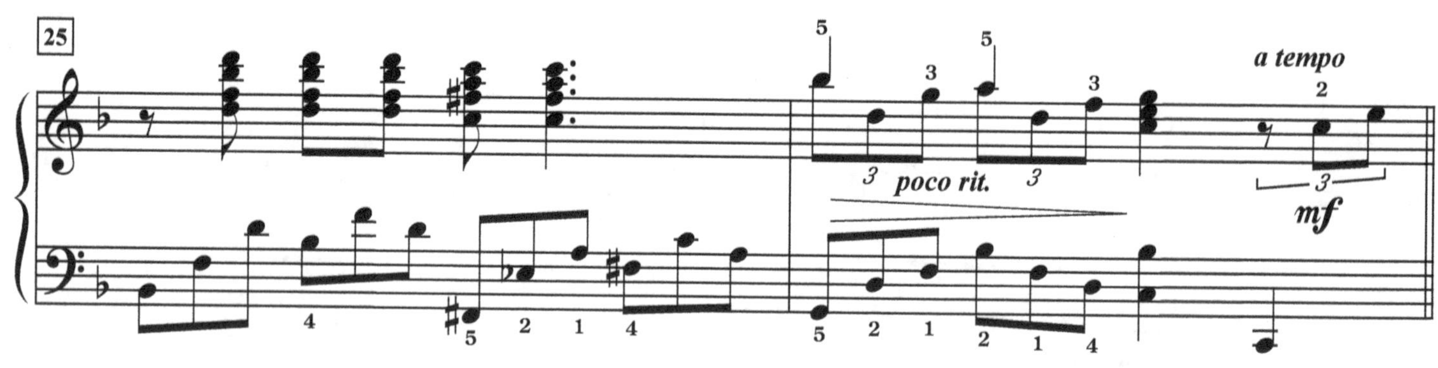
25
poco rit.
a tempo
mf

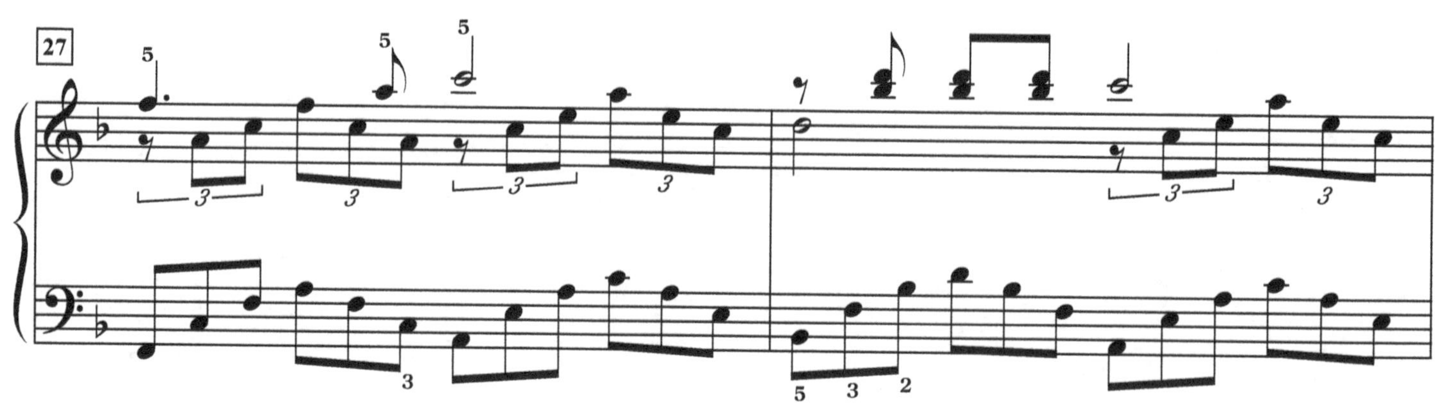
27

29

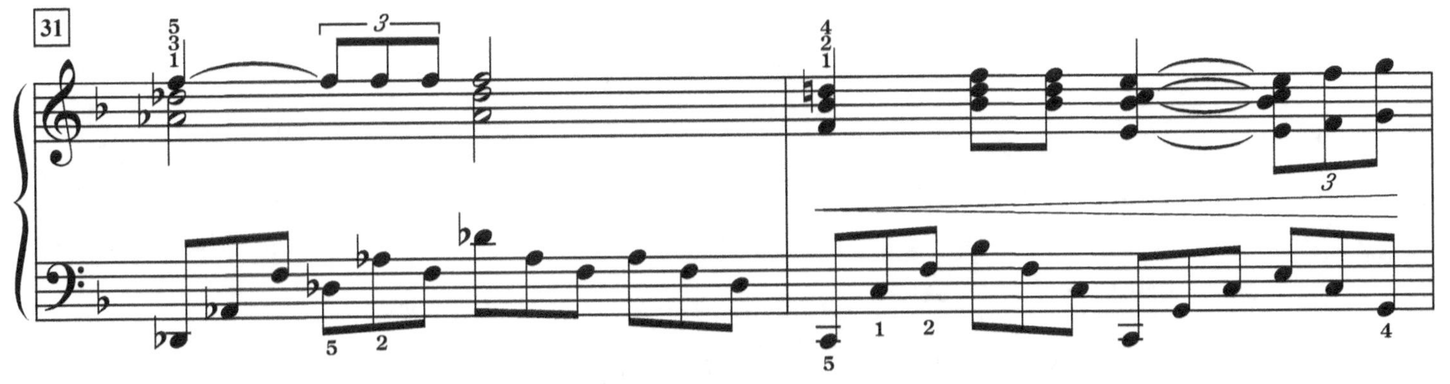
31

33
f

35

37
mf
rit.
mp

Celebrate Me Home

Lyrics by Kenny Loggins
Music by Kenny Loggins and Bob James
Arranged by Dan Coates

17

21
mf

25

29
f

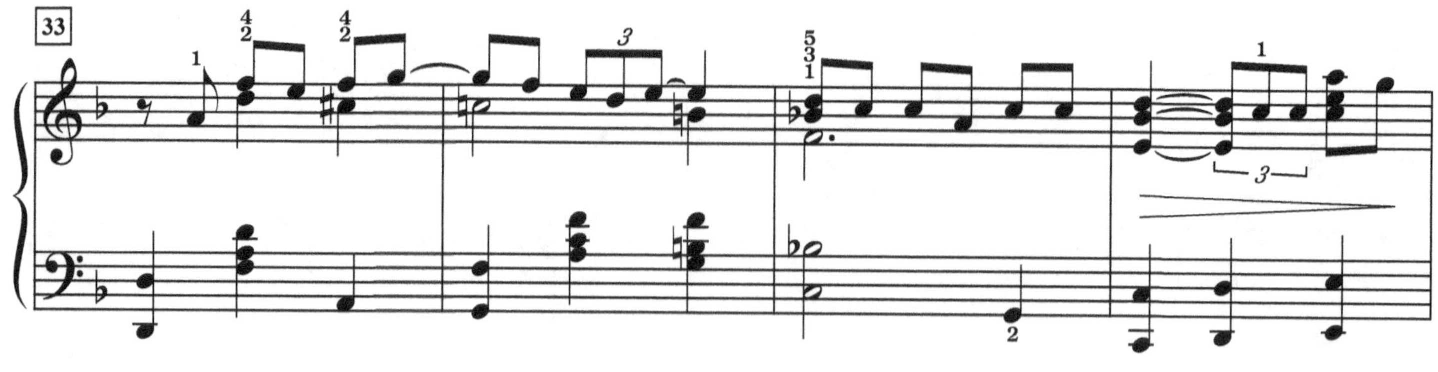
33
1
4
2
4
2
3
5
3
1
2
1
3

37
mf
3
5
1
3
2

41
1
mp
3
1
4
5
1
3

45
2
3
5
1
2–1

49
cresc.

53
mf
f

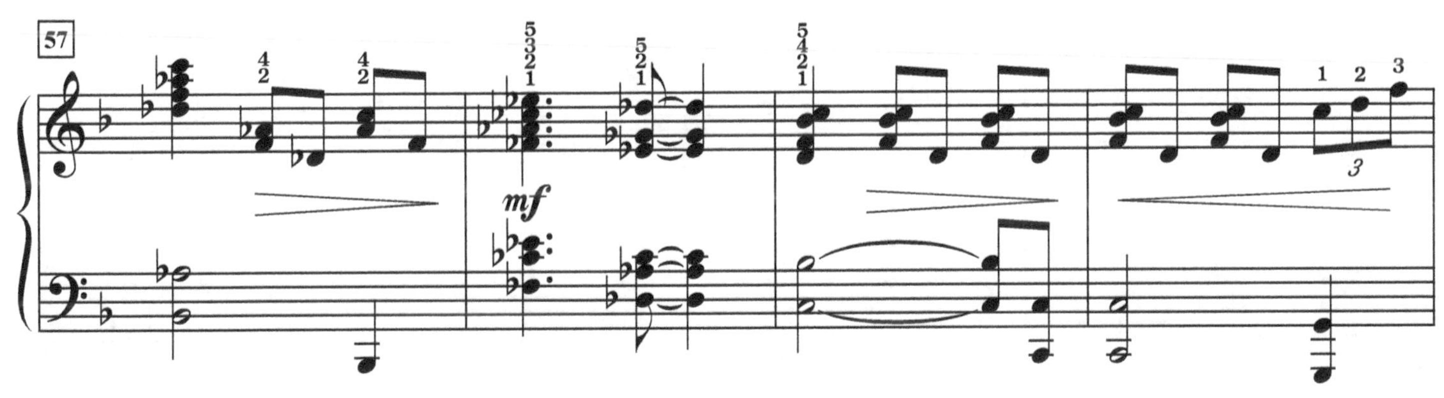
57
mf

61
f

65

69

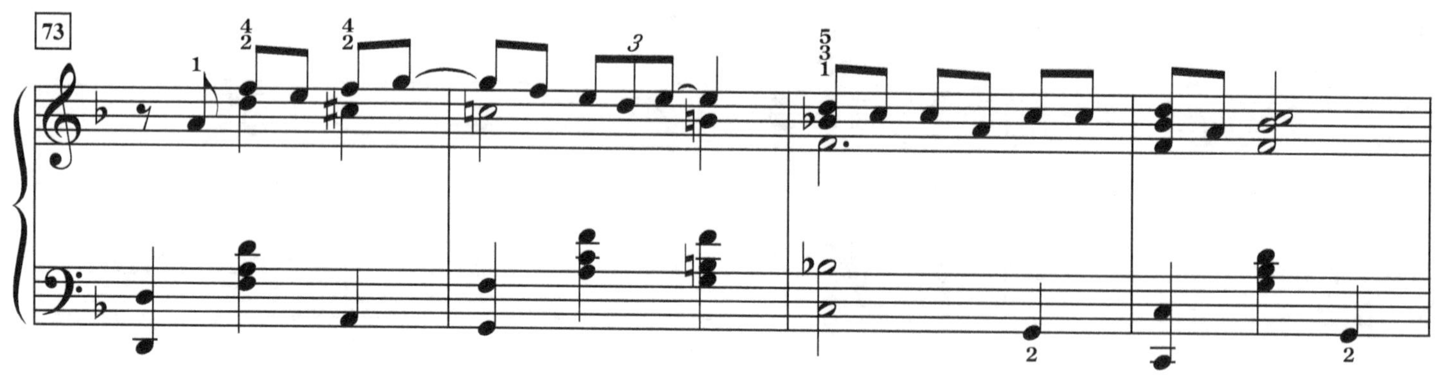
73

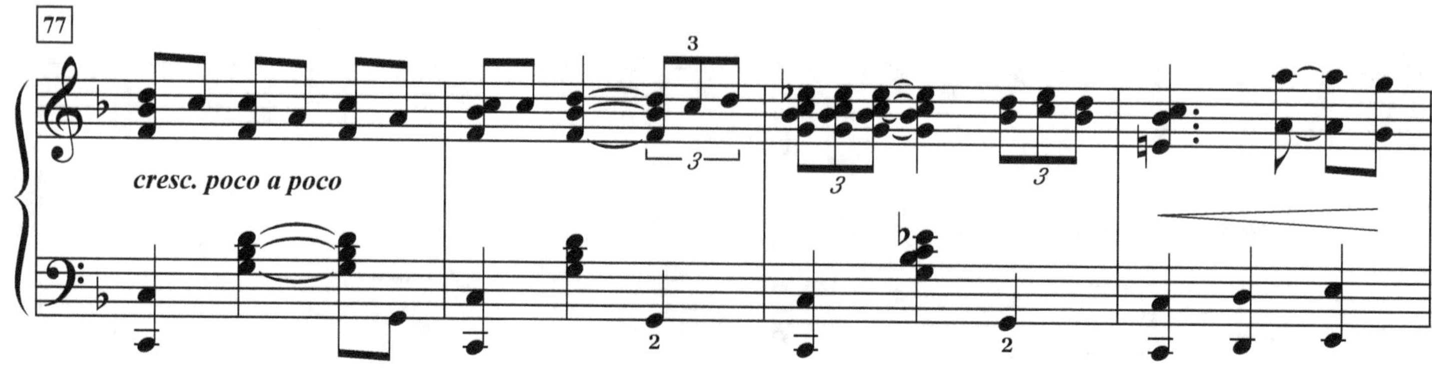
77
cresc. poco a poco

81
ff

85

89
mf
play 3 times

93
f
mf
molto rit.
mp

KILLING ME SOFTLY

Words and Music by
Charles Fox and Norman Gimbel
Arranged by Dan Coates

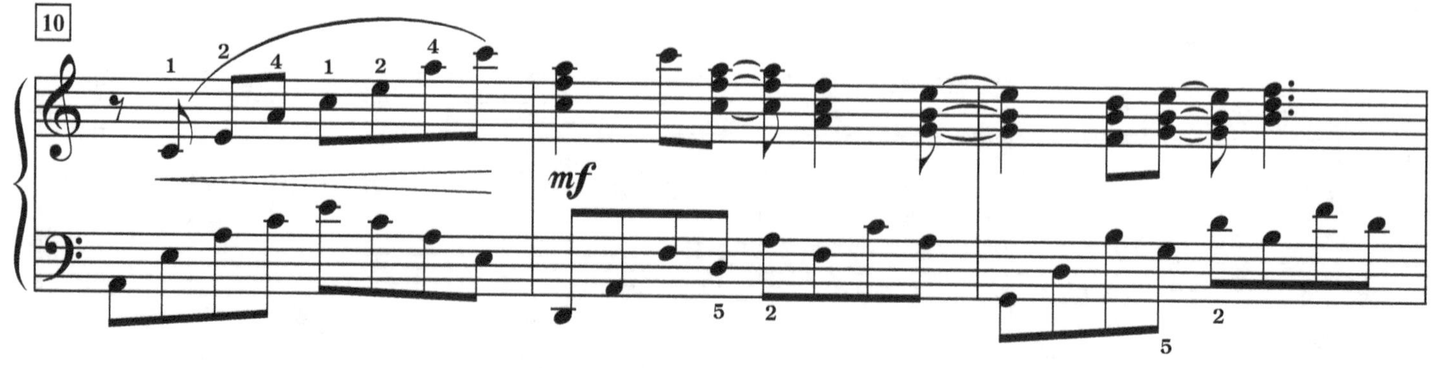

13
16
19
22
25
f
dim.
mf
to Coda
1.

2.
29
31
34
37
40
D.S. al Coda
mp

Coda
46
49
52
55
mp rit.
Ballads

Let Me Fall
(from Cirque du Soleil's *Quidam*)

Words by Jim Corcoran
Music by Benoit Jutras
Arranged by Dan Coates

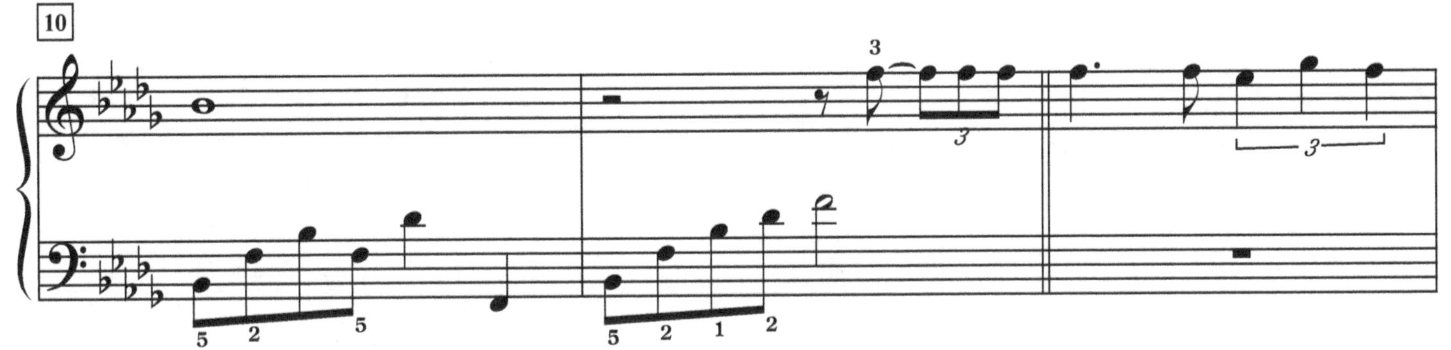

Ballads

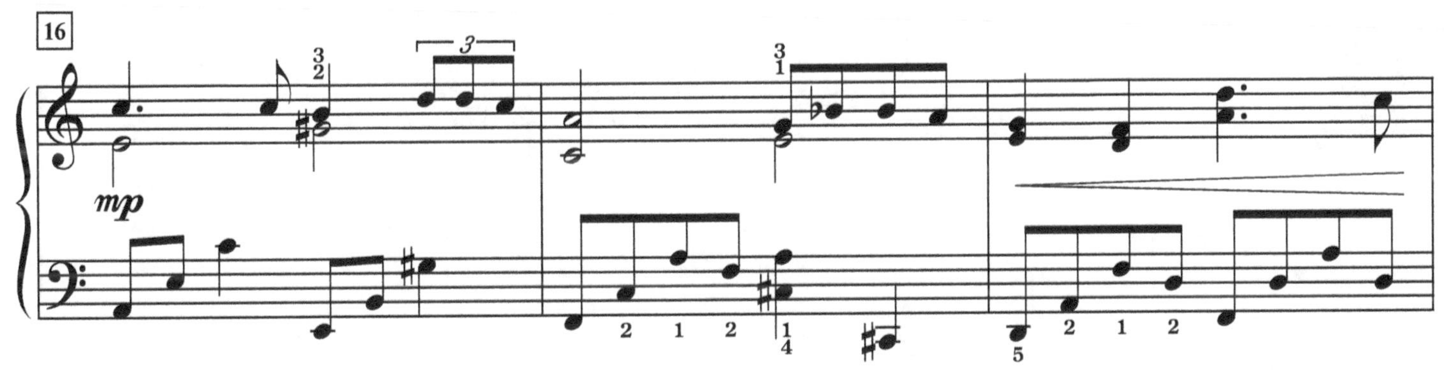

22
25
mf
28
8va
mf
31
8va
f

34
mf

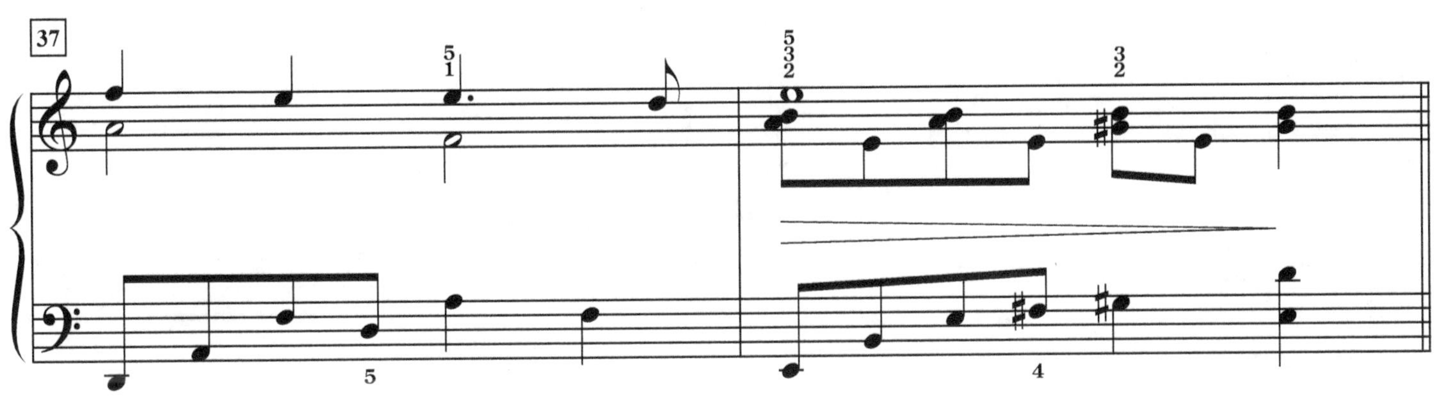
37

39
mp

41

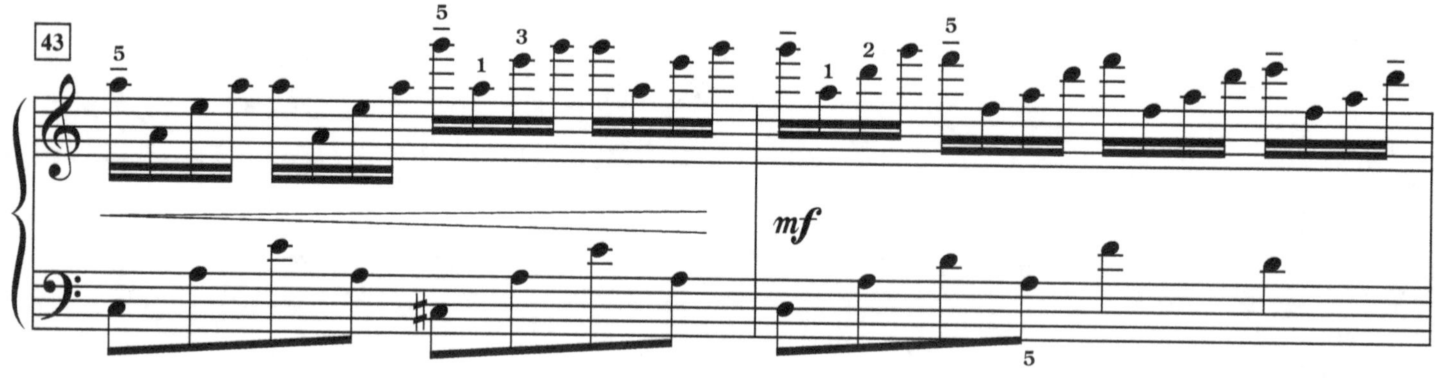
43
mf

45
mp
cresc.

48
f
8va

51
mf
mp

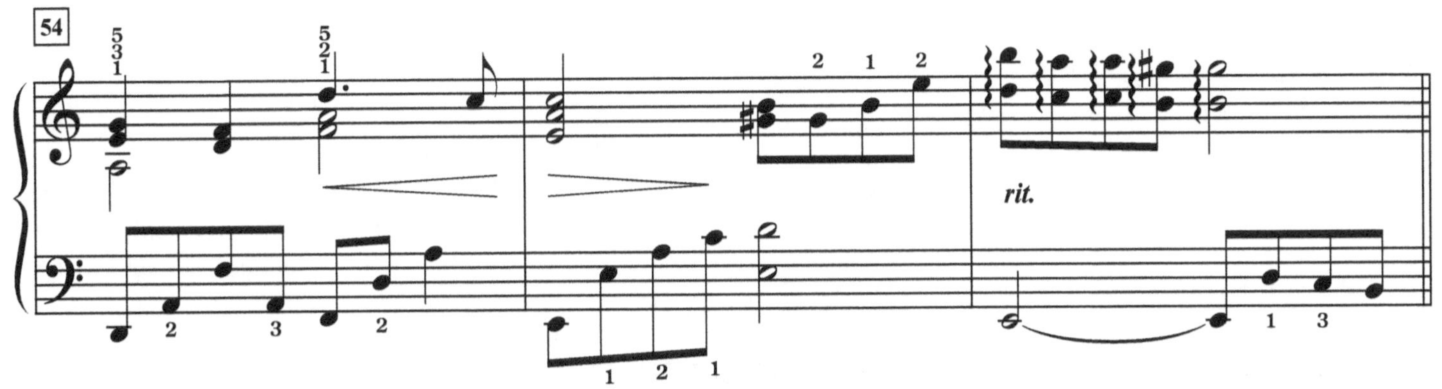
54
rit.

57
a tempo
mp

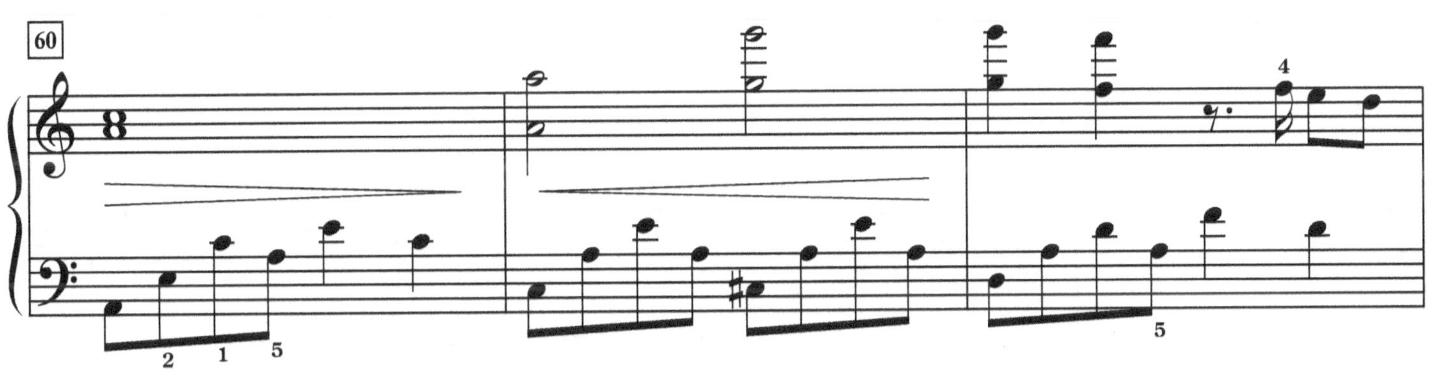
60

63
rit.
p

Secret Love
(from *Calamity Jane*)

Words by Paul Francis Webster
Music by Sammy Fain
Arranged by Dan Coates

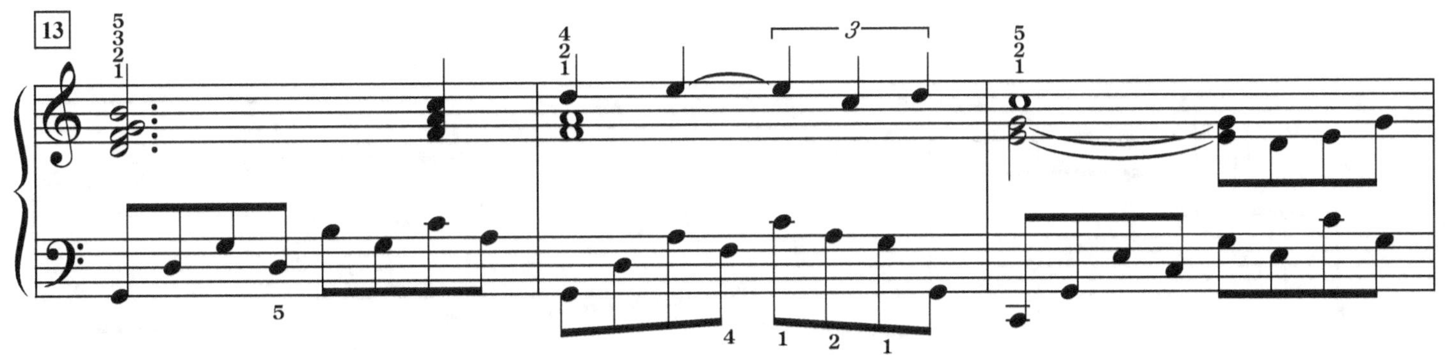

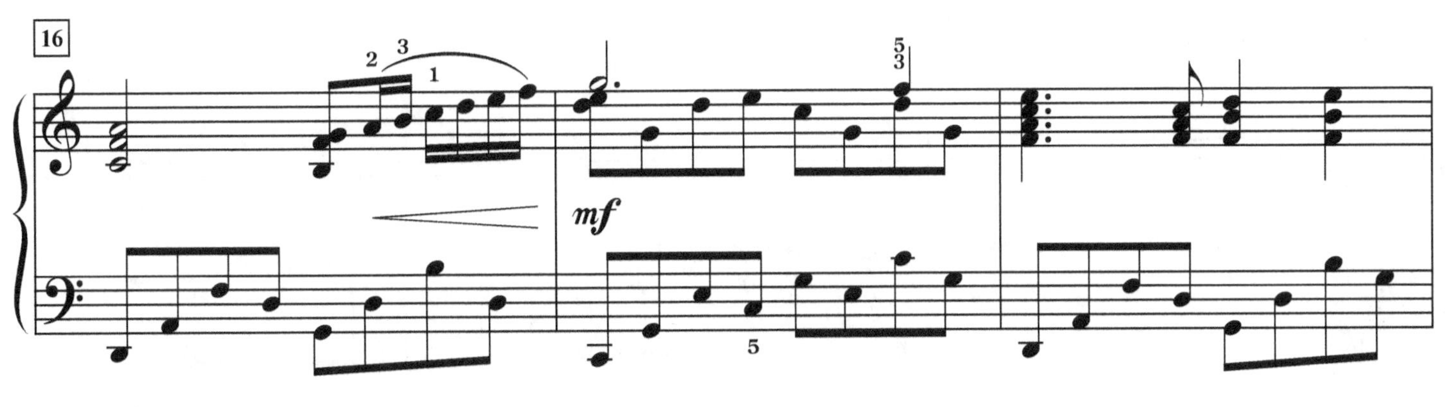

Ballads

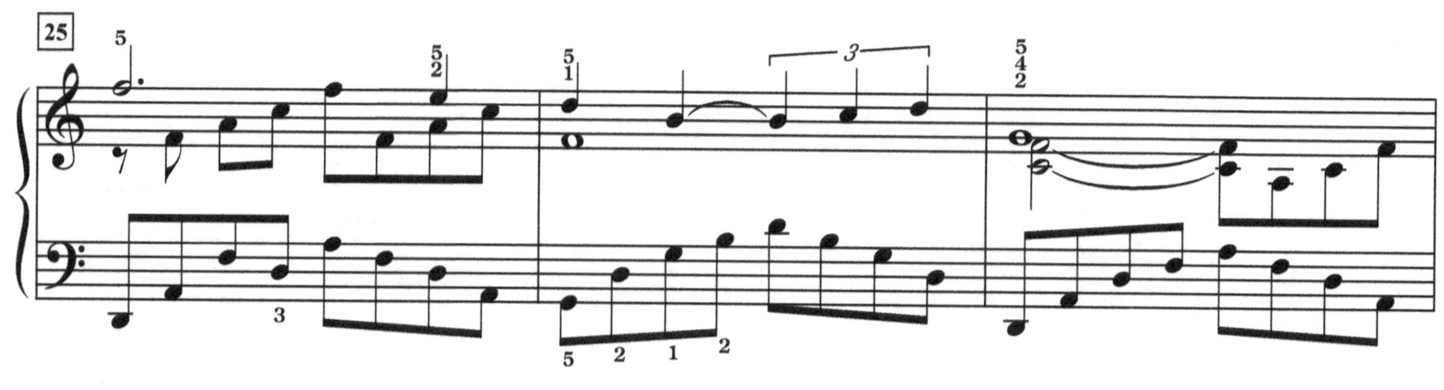
25
5
5
2
5
1
3
5
4
2
3
5 2 1 2

28
4
2
1
5
3
1
2 1 2 1

31
2 3 4 1 2
3
f
2

34
3
5
3
2

37
40
mf
43
46
1.
49
2.
mp
rit.
8va
p

The Shadow of Your Smile

(from *The Sandpiper*)

Lyric by Paul Francis Webster
Music by Johnny Mandel
Arranged by Dan Coates

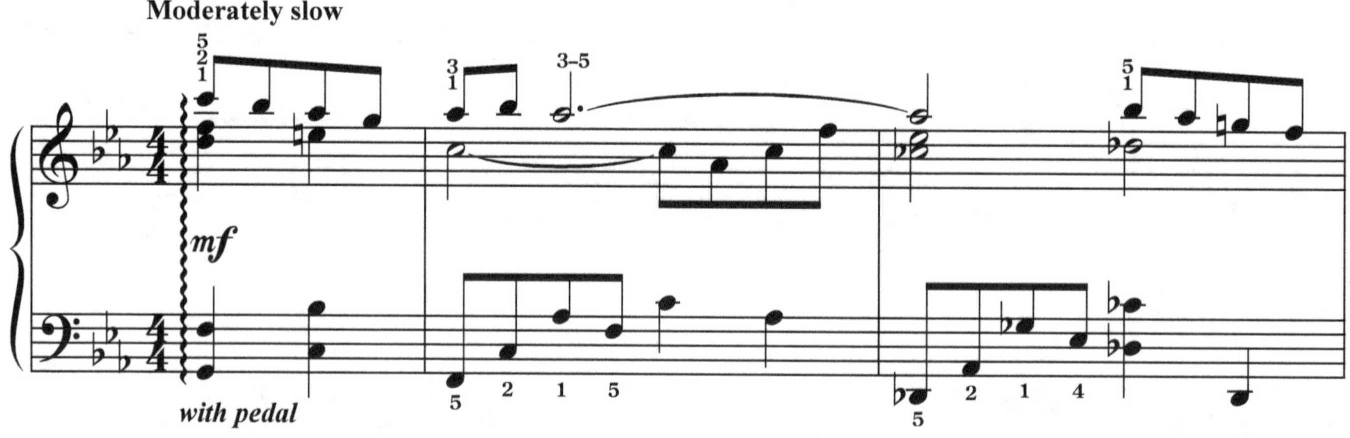

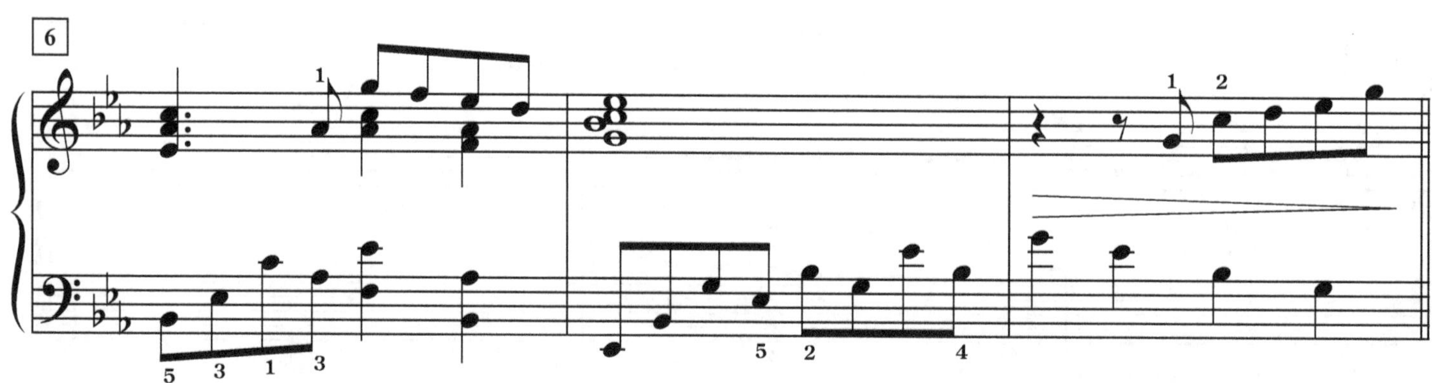

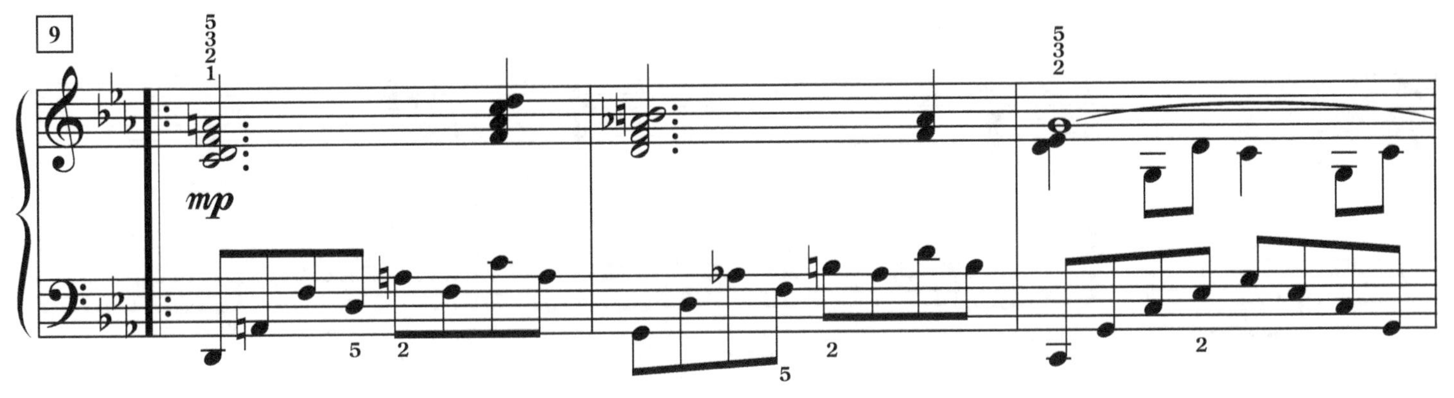
9
mp

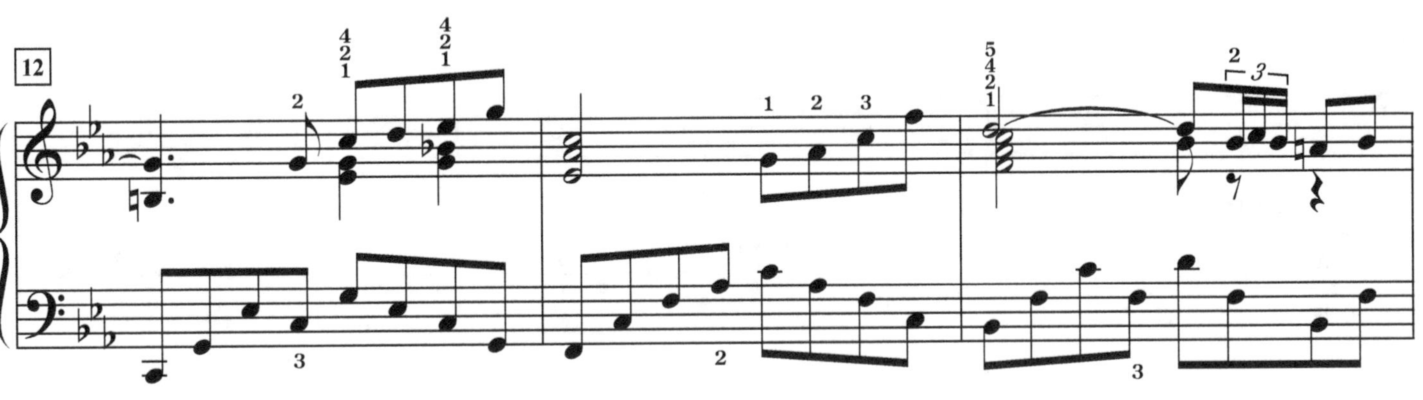
12

15
mf

18

21

24
mp
mf

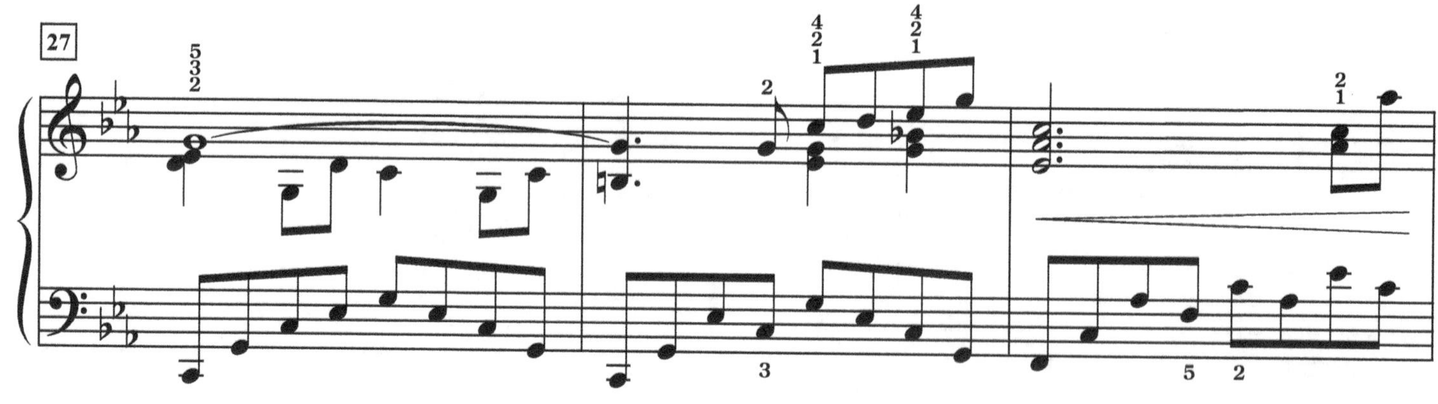
27

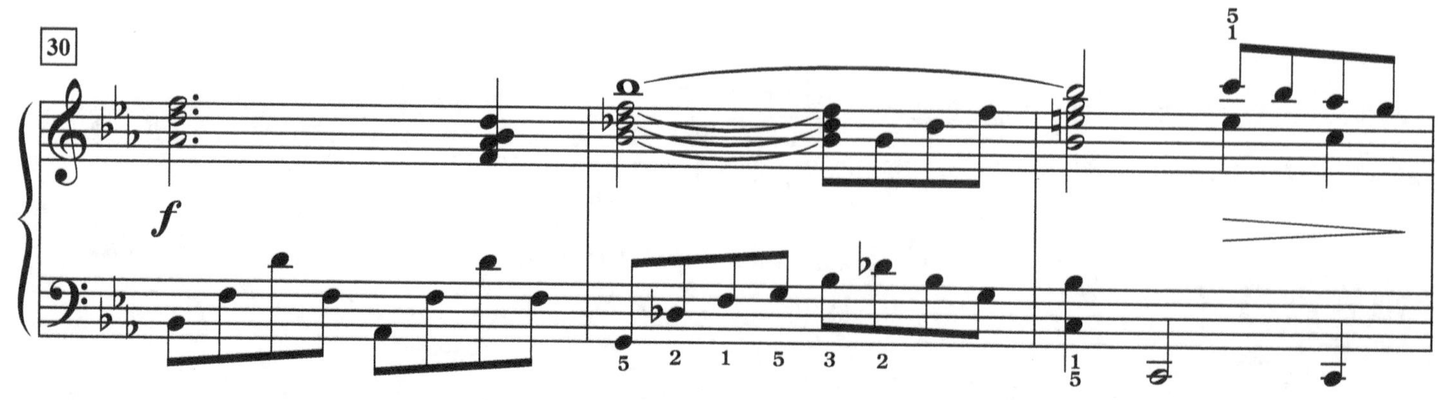
30
f

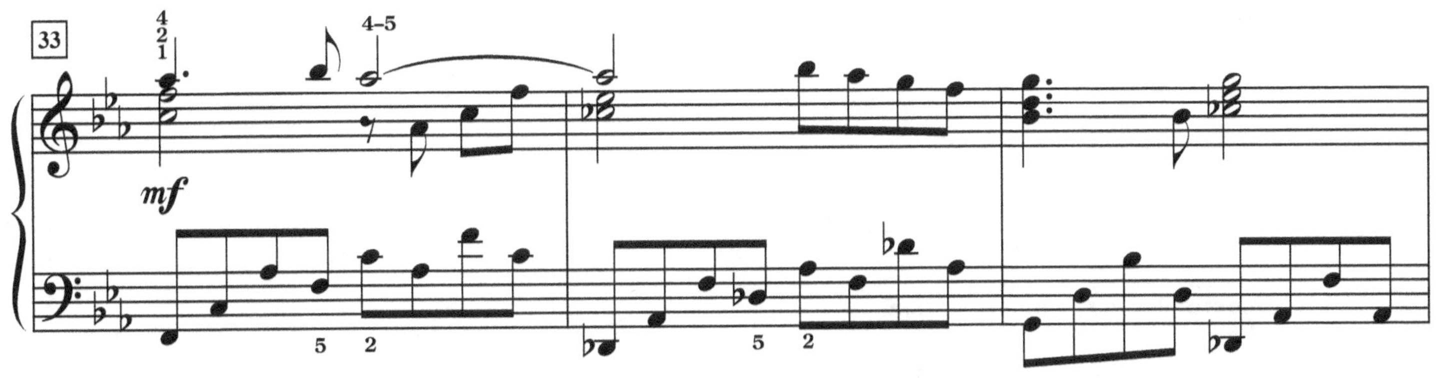
33
mf

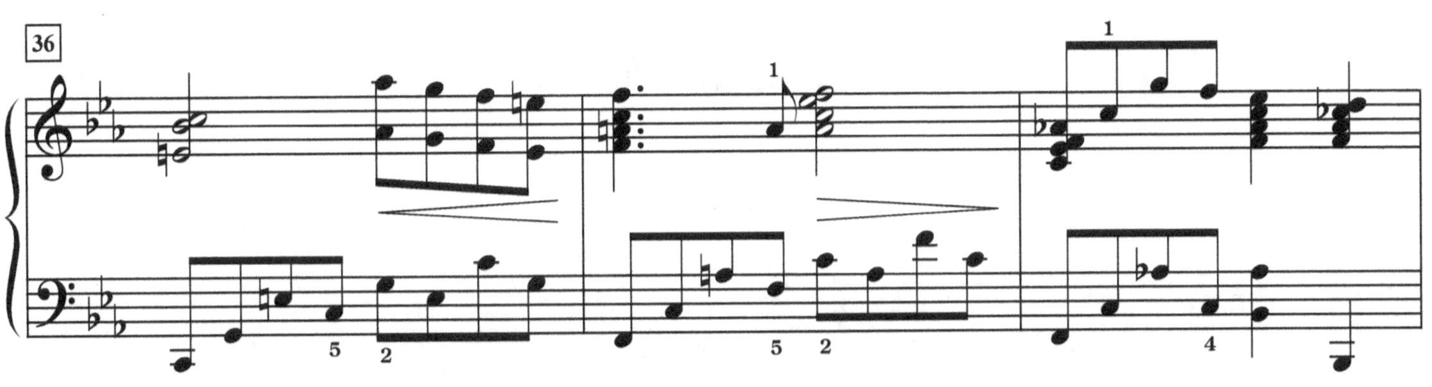
36

39
1.
2.

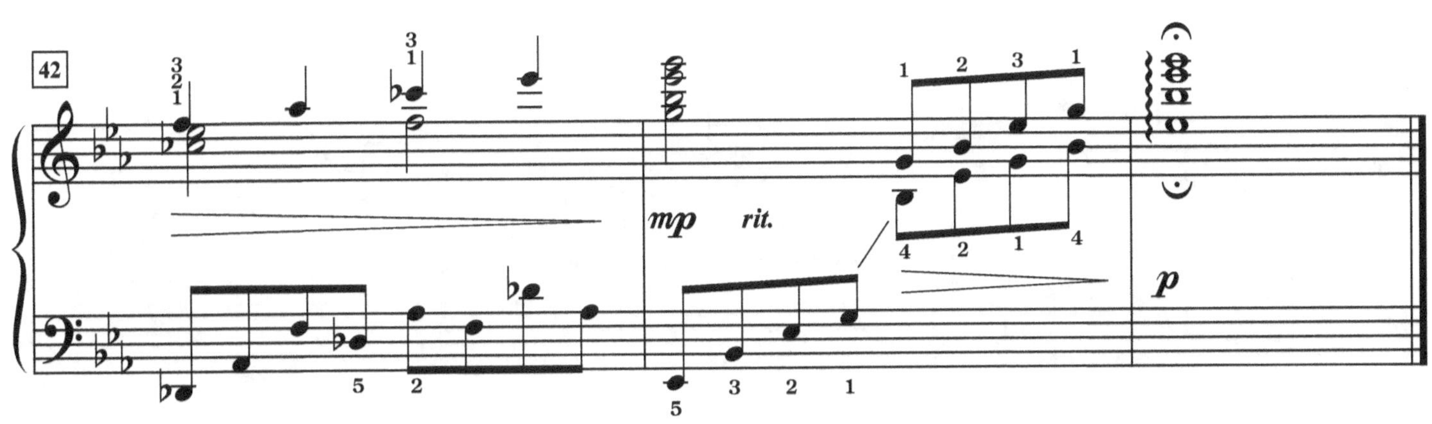
42
mp
rit.
p

Someone to Watch Over Me
(from *Oh, Kay!*)

Music and Lyrics by
George Gershwin and Ira Gershwin
Arranged by Dan Coates

12

15
mf

18

21
dim.

24
mp
f

27

29
mf
1.

32
mp
2.
rit.
mp

Somewhere My Love (Lara's Theme)

(from *Doctor Zhivago*)

By Maurice Jarre
Arranged by Dan Coates

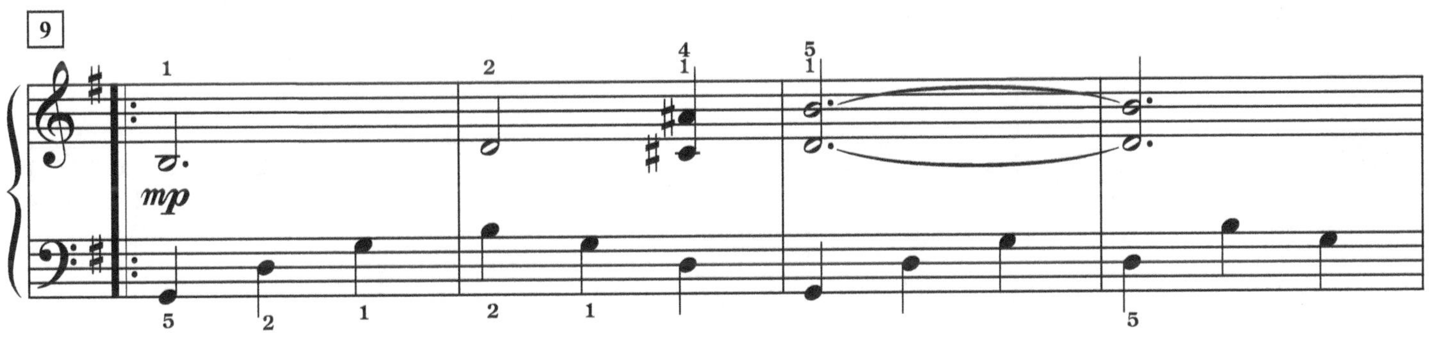

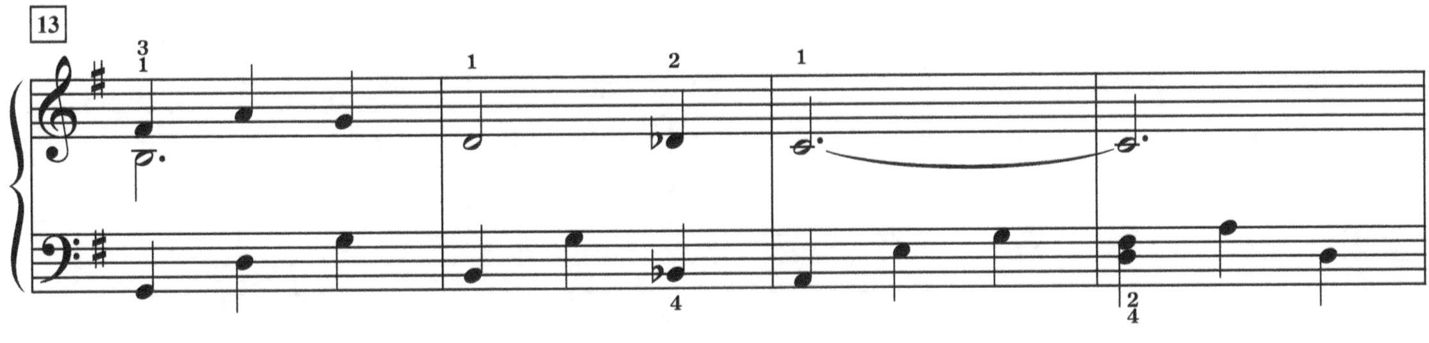

Ballads

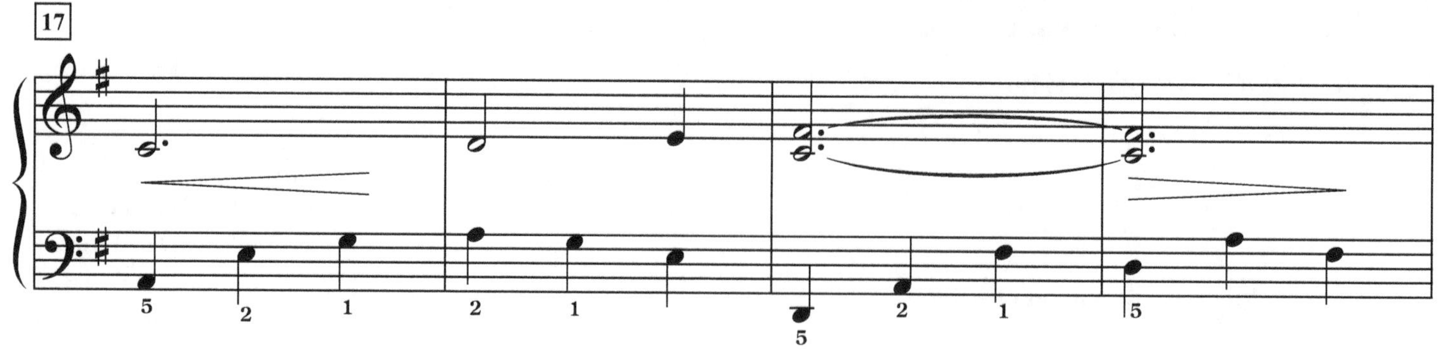
17

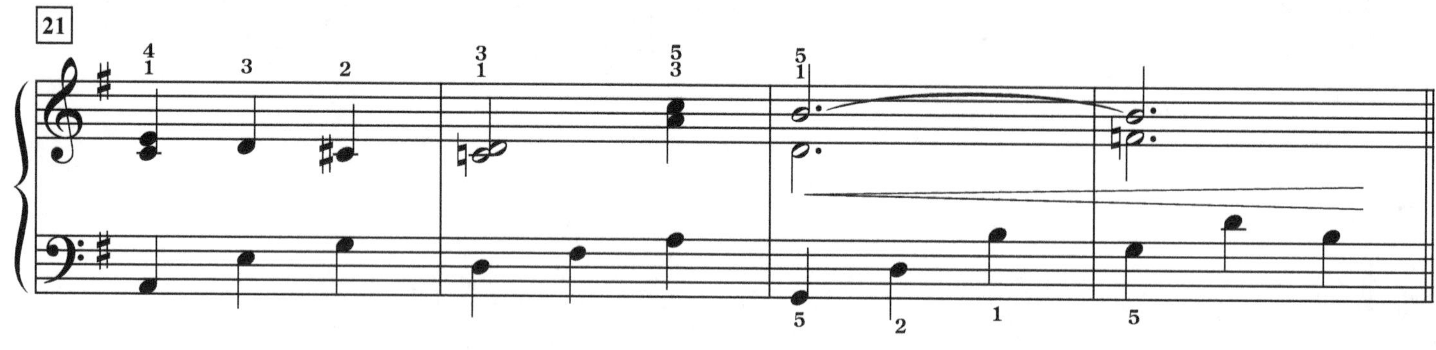
21

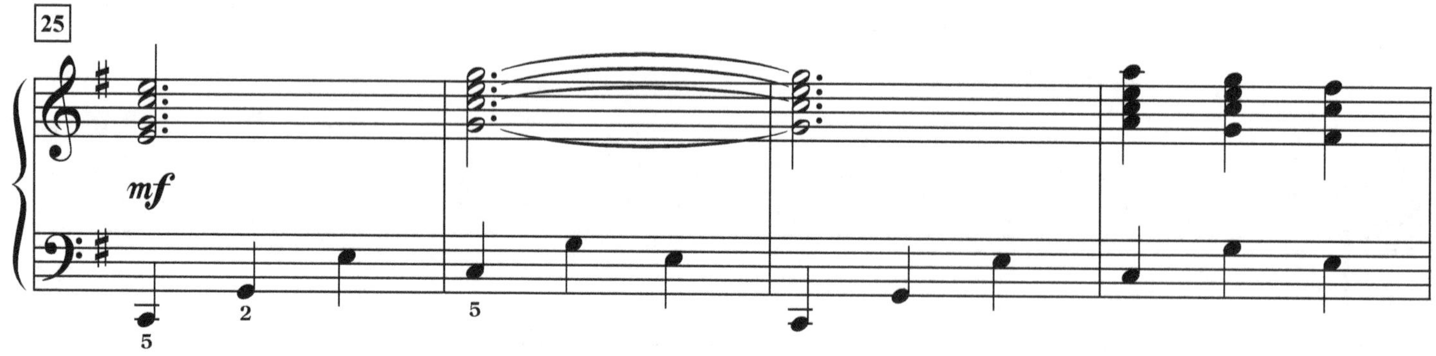
25
mf

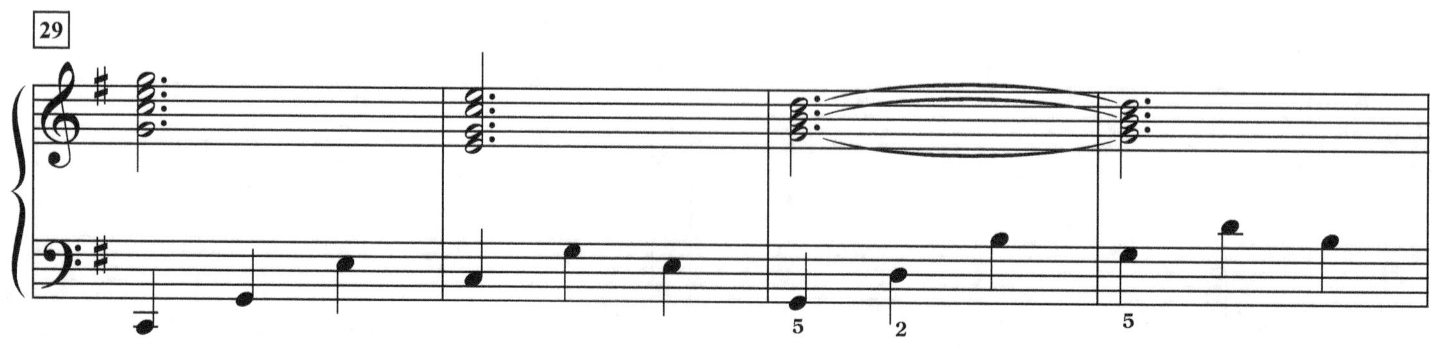
29

33
5
2
5
5
3
2

37
4
f
4
2
1–2
3
5

41
mf

45
3
2
1
5
1
4
5
4

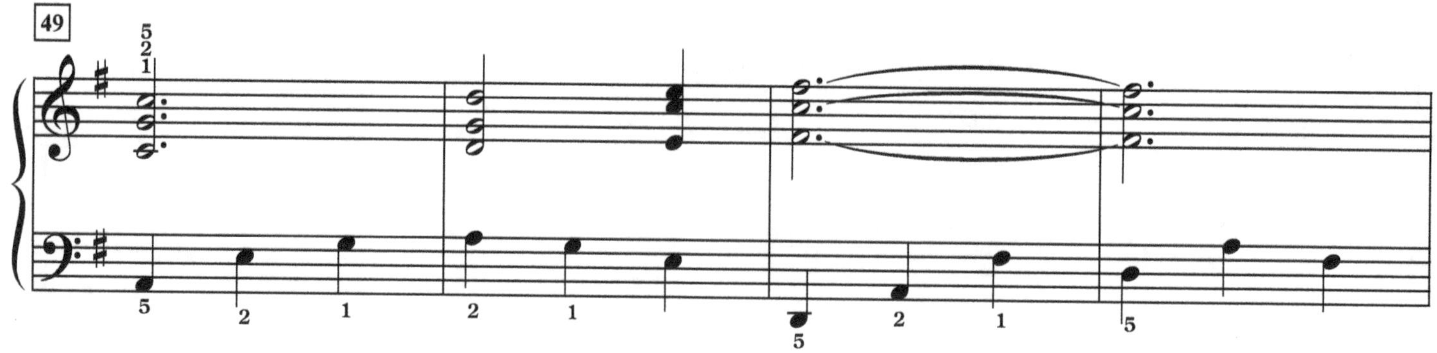
49

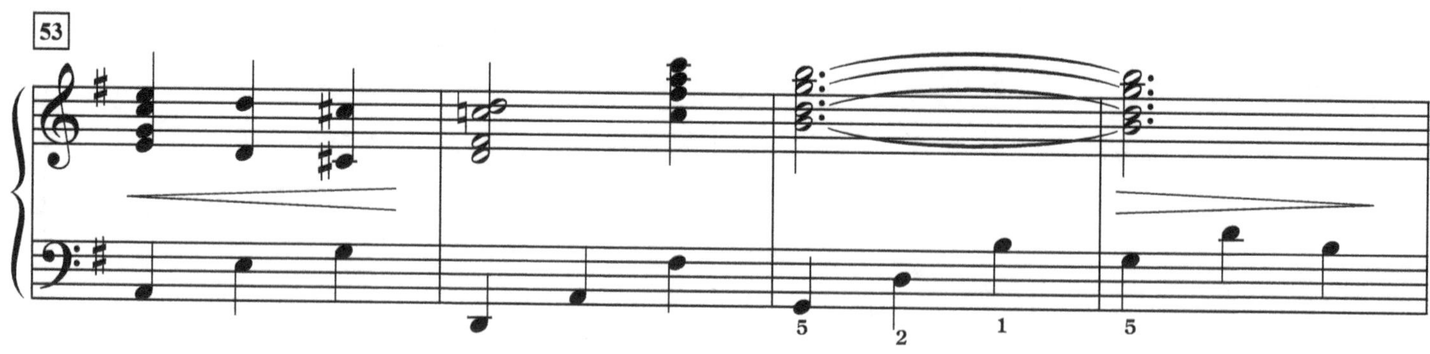
53

57

61

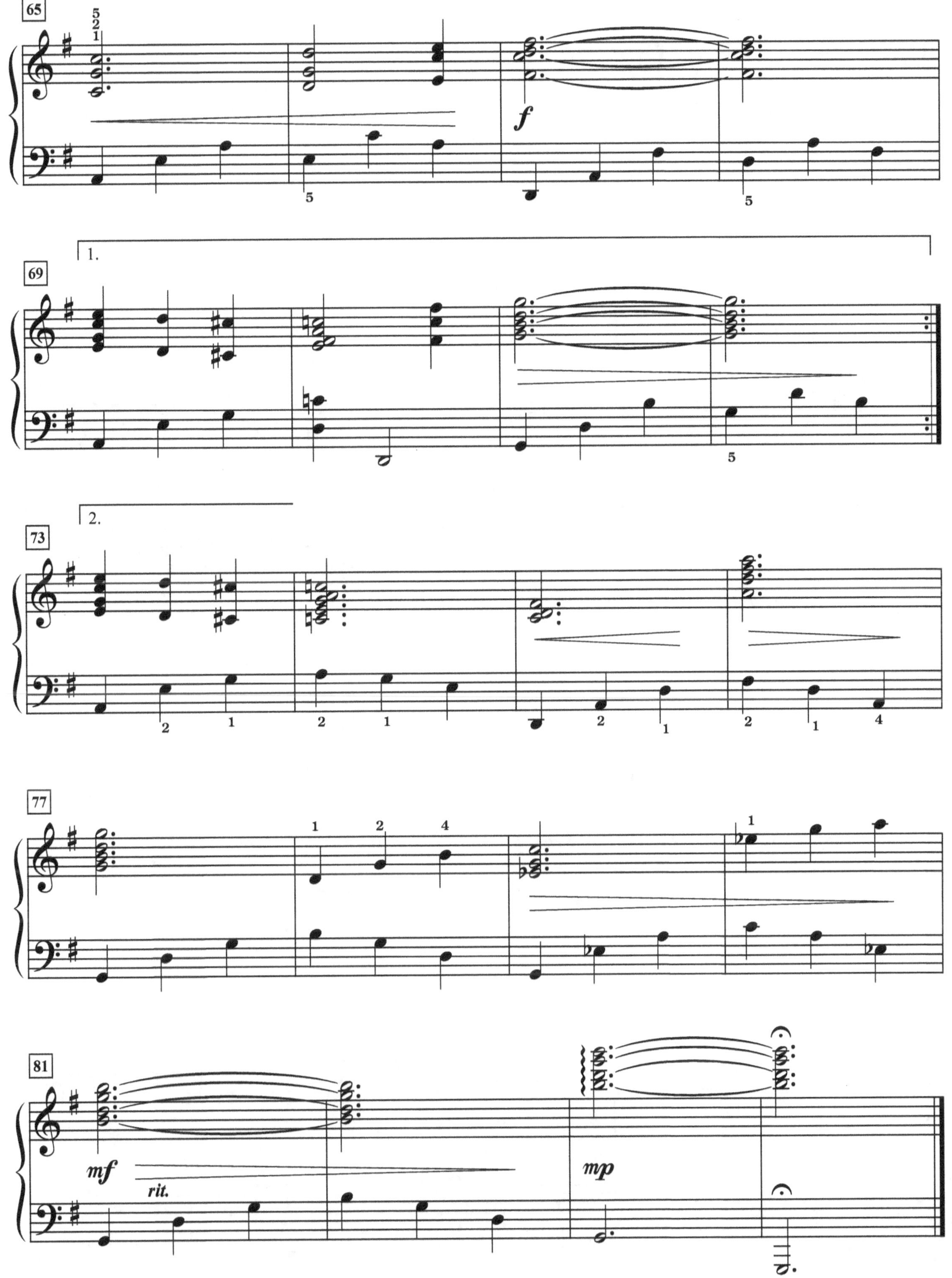
65
69
1.
73
2.
77
81
f
mf
rit.
mp

To Make You Feel My Love

Words and Music by Bob Dylan
Arranged by Dan Coates

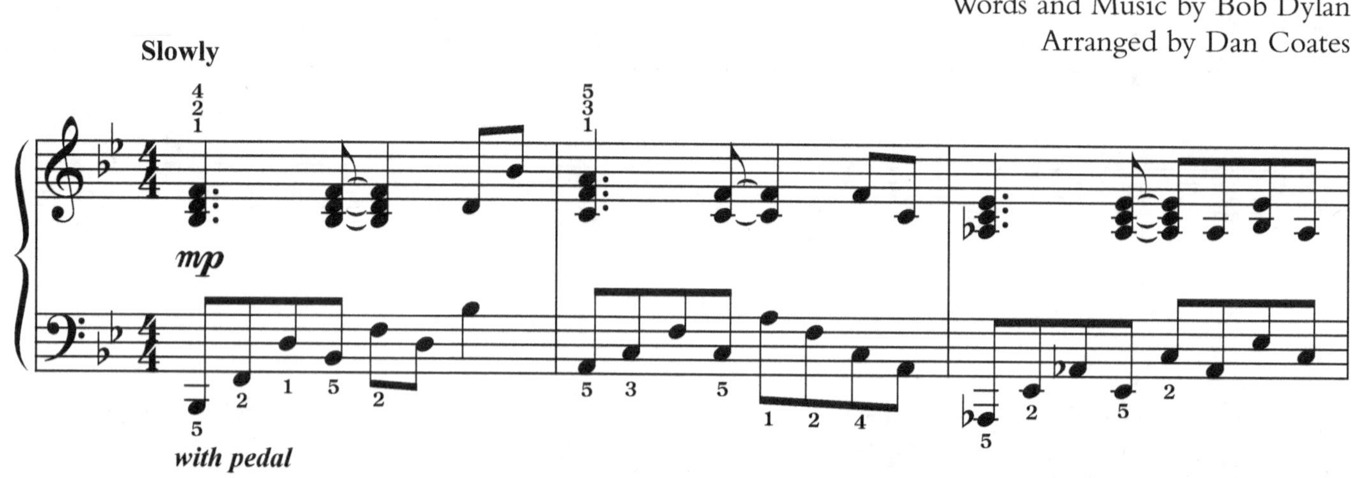

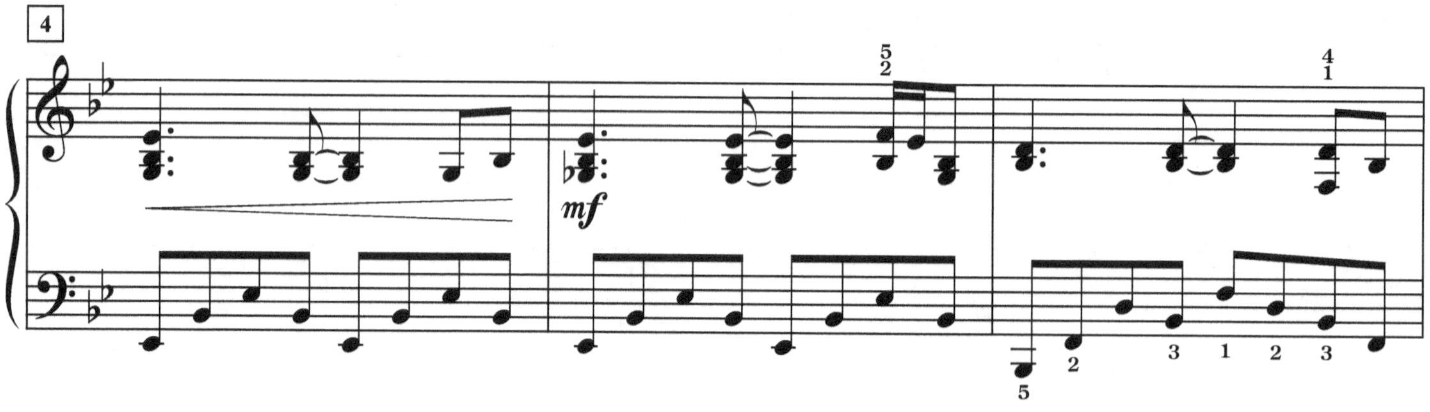

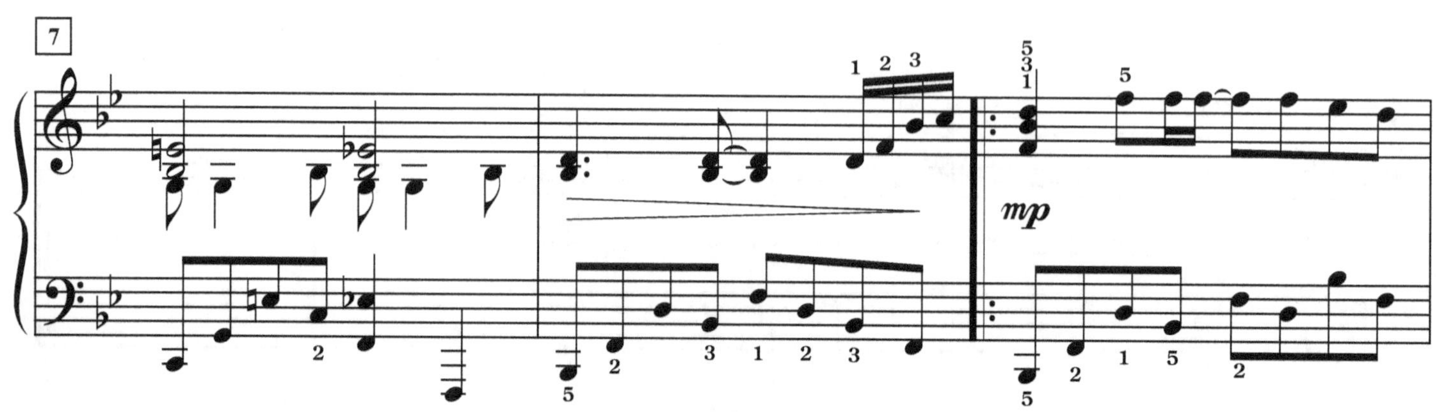

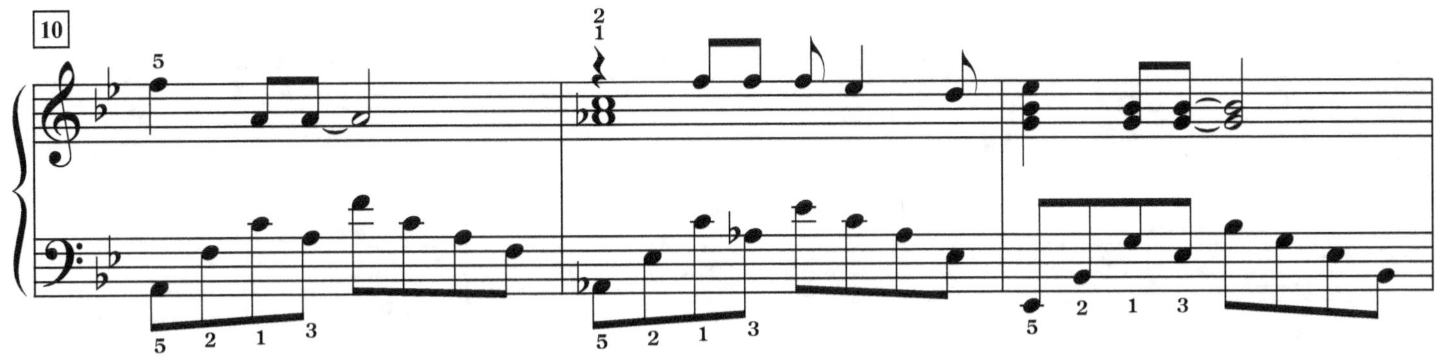
10

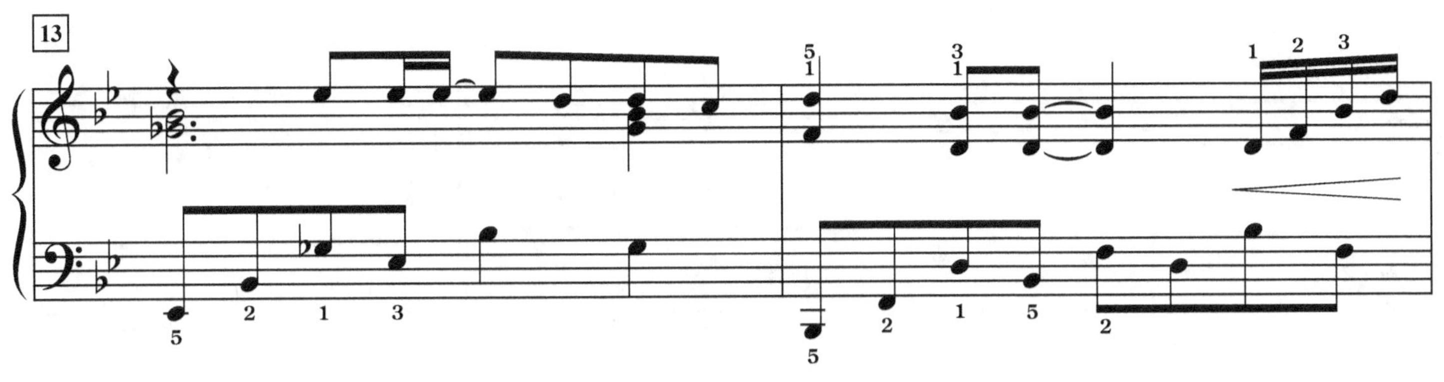
13

15
1.
2.

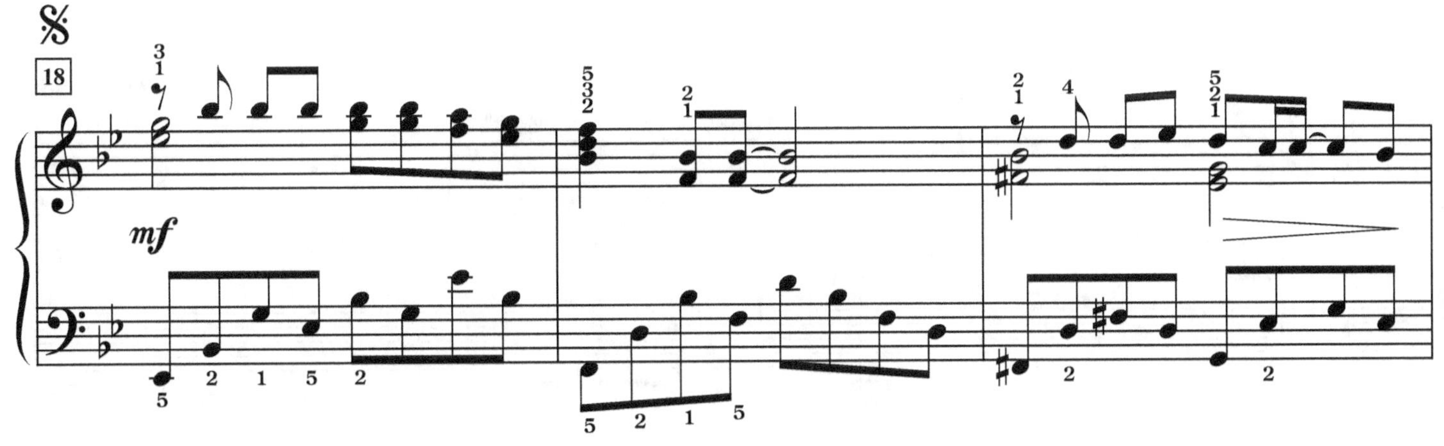
18
mf

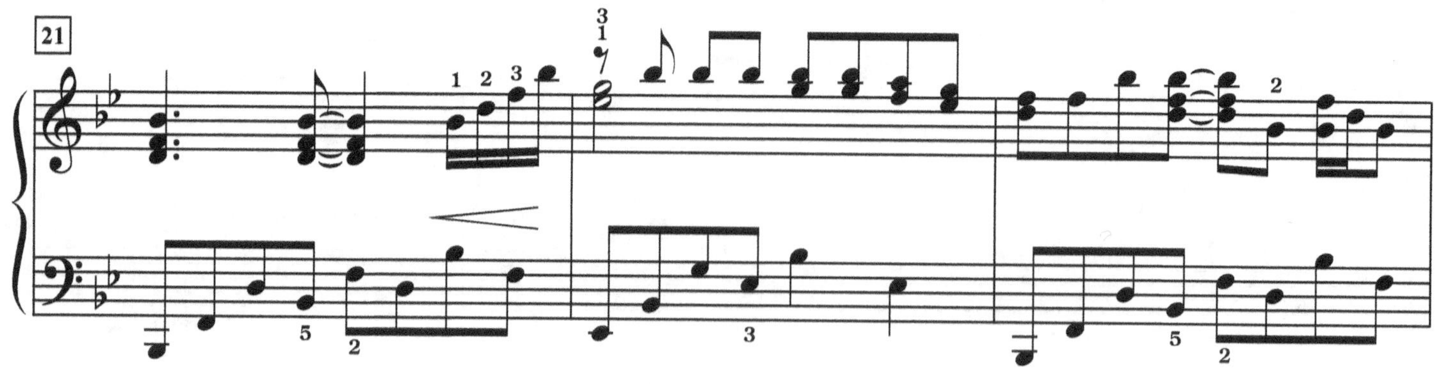
21

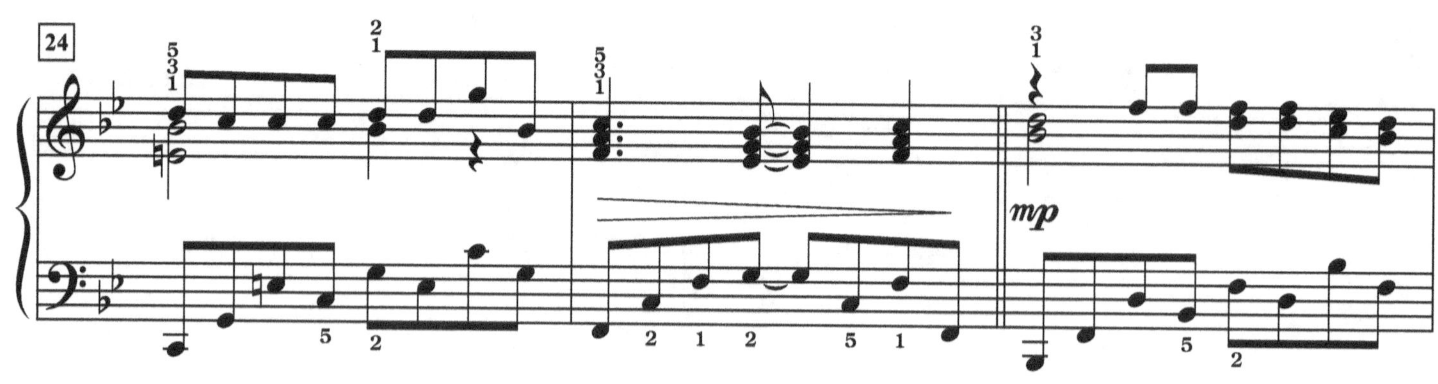
24
mp

27

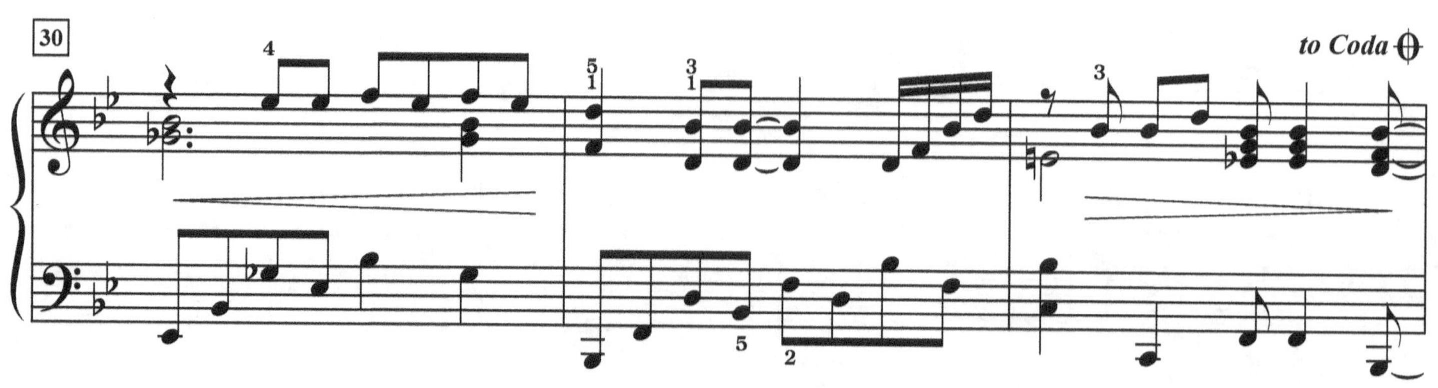
30
to Coda

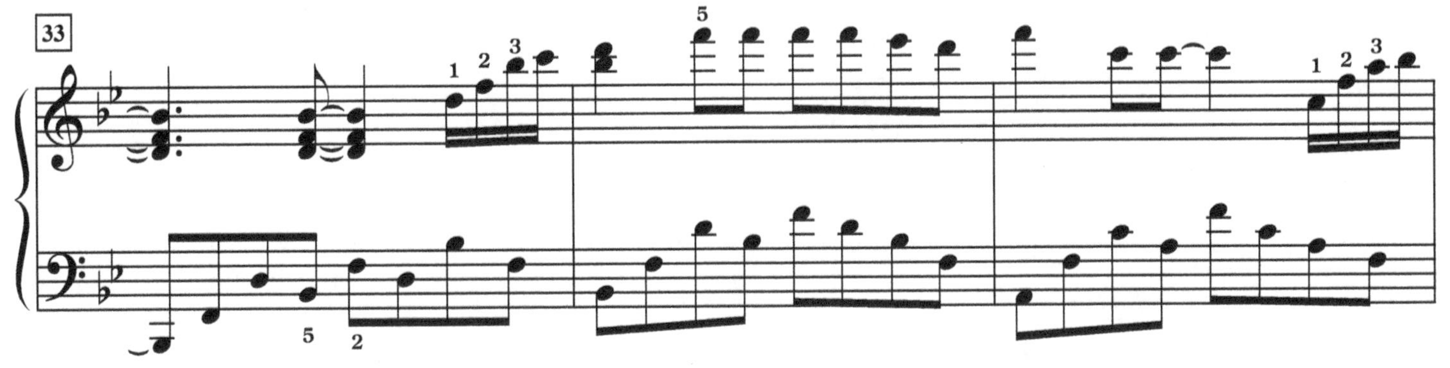
33

36

39
D.S. al Coda

Coda
rit.

True Love
(from *High Society*)

Words and Music by Cole Porter
Arranged by Dan Coates

17
5
2
5

21
mf

25

29
mp

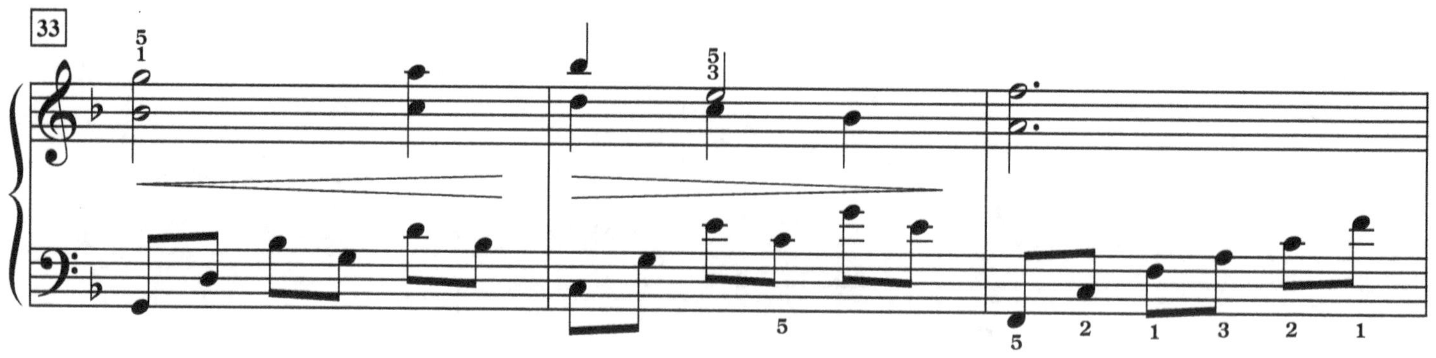
33
5
1
5
3
5
5
2
1
3
2
1

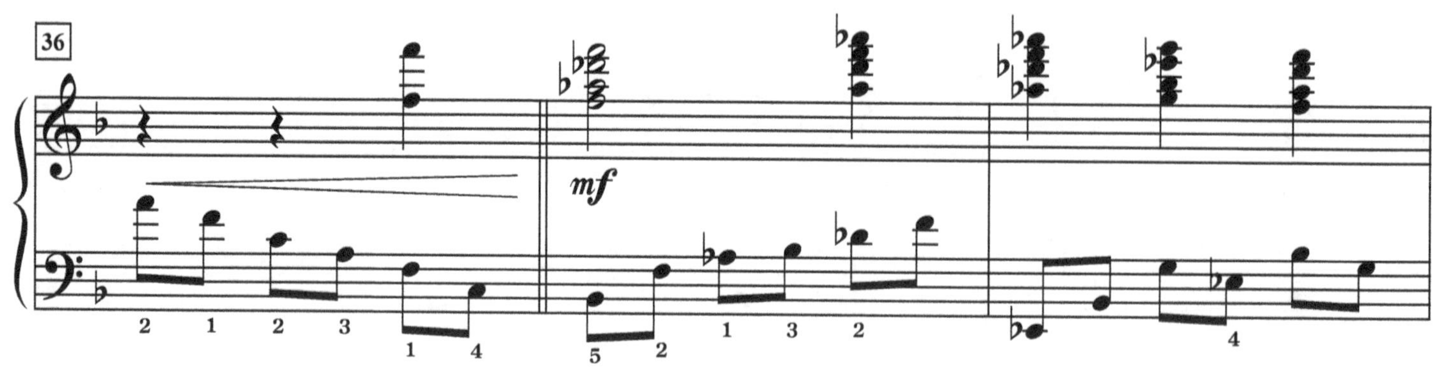
36
mf
2
1
2
3
1
4
5
2
1
3
2
4

39

42
5
3
1
2
1
4

45
5
3
1
mp

48
5
mf

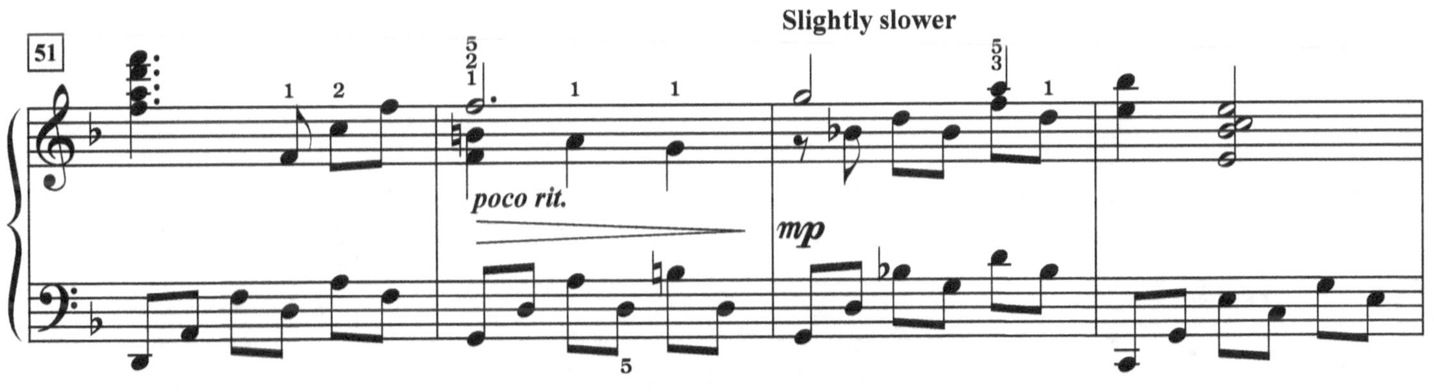
51
1 2
5
2
1
1 1
poco rit.
5
Slightly slower
5
3
1
mp

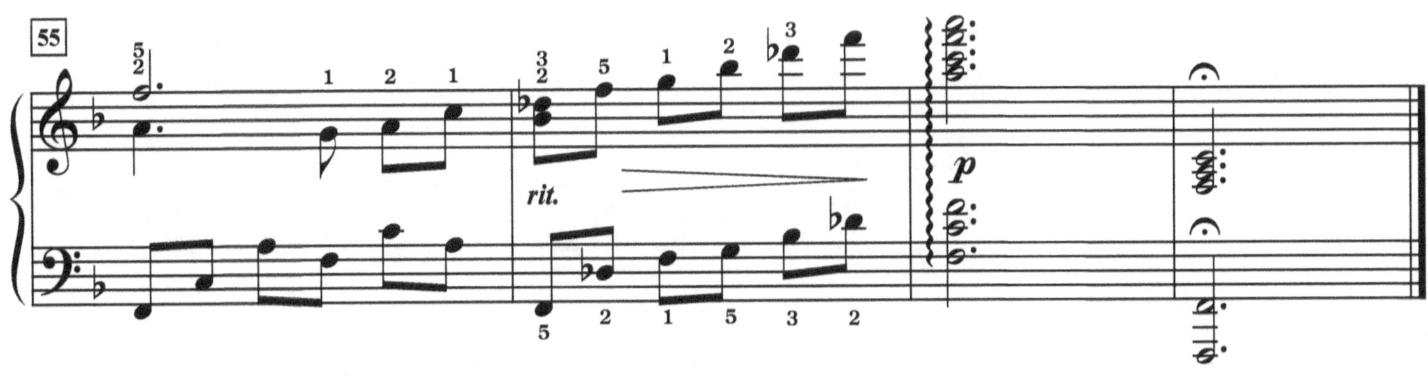
55
5
2
1 2 1
3
2
5 1 2 3
rit.
5 2 1 5 3 2
p

The Colors of the Wind
(from *Pocahontas*)

Lyrics by Stephen Schwartz
Music by Alan Menken
Arranged by Dan Coates

16
19
1.
f espressivo
22
cresc.
25
ff
f
28
mf

31
8va
mp
34
2.
f
37
cresc. poco a poco
rit.
40
Broadly
ff
42
simile

44
dim. poco a poco
46
8va
mf
48
cresc. poco a poco
50
a tempo
ff
rit.
mf
52
8va
mp
rit.
p
pp

A Dream Is a Wish Your Heart Makes

(from *Cinderella*)

Words and Music by
Mack David, Al Hoffman and Jerry Livingston
Arranged by Dan Coates

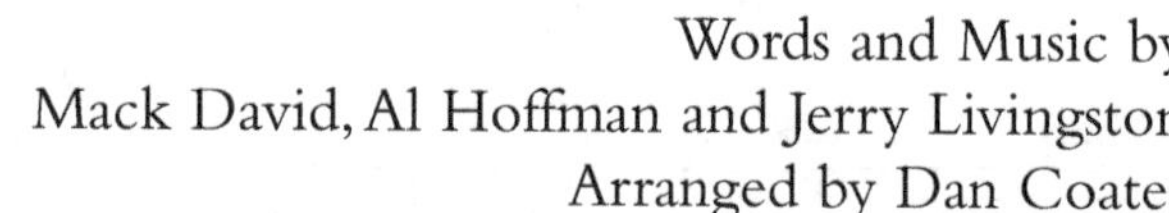

Slowly, with expression

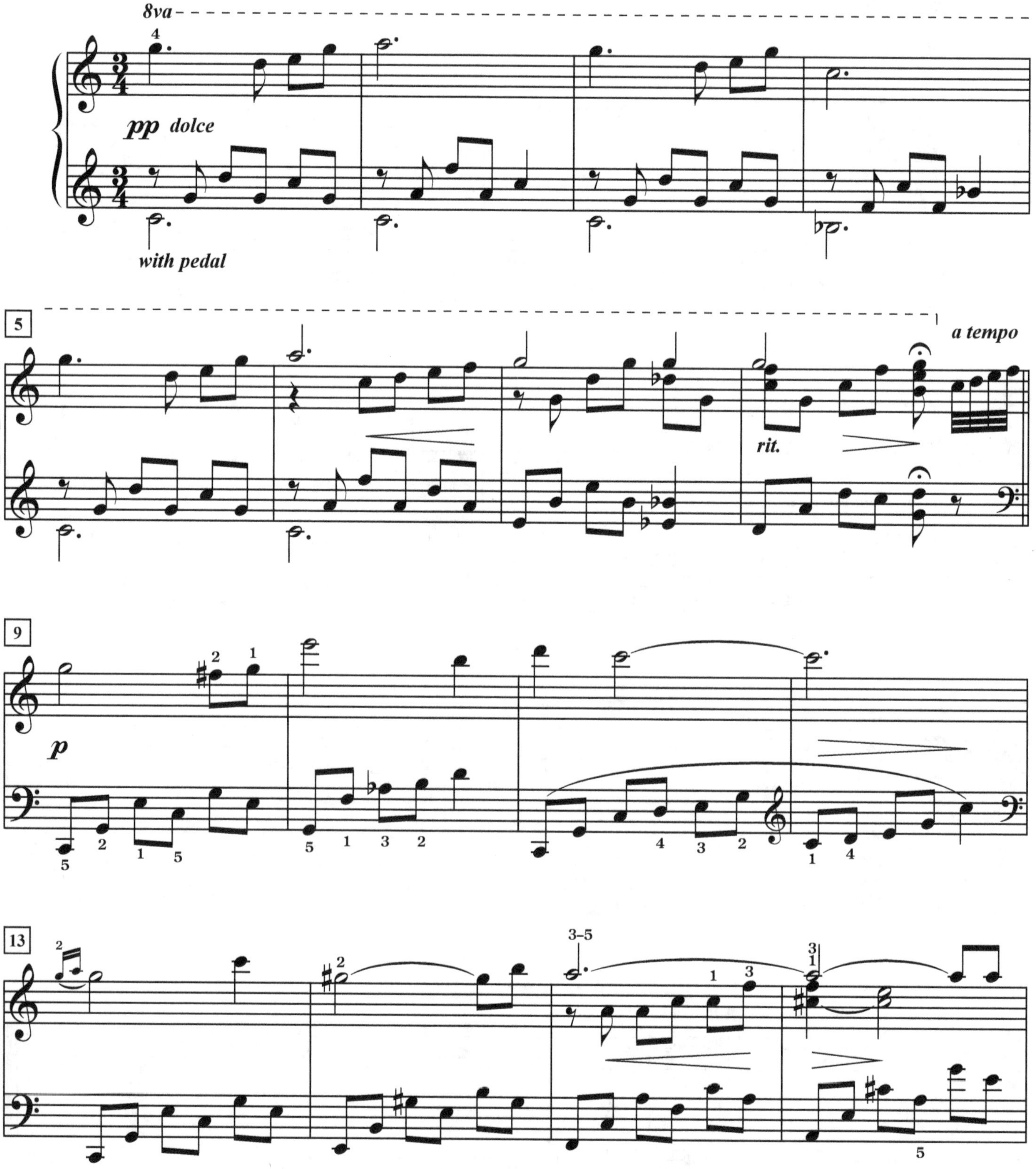

8va
pp dolce
with pedal
5
a tempo
rit.
9
p
13

17
mp
21
25
8va
mf
poco accel.
8va
29
Suddenly slower
rit.
33
Tempo I
f

37
mp legato
rit.
a tempo
39
fz
mp
cresc. poco a poco
41
8va
43
ff
8va
dim.
8va
45
8va
mf
rit.

Slower
47
mp lightly
49
51
mf
rit.
Meno mosso
53
mp
8va
55
p molto rit. e dim.
pp
ppp

Movie Solos

Days of Wine and Roses
(from *Days of Wine and Roses*)

Lyric by Johnny Mercer
Music by Henry Mancini
Arranged by Dan Coates

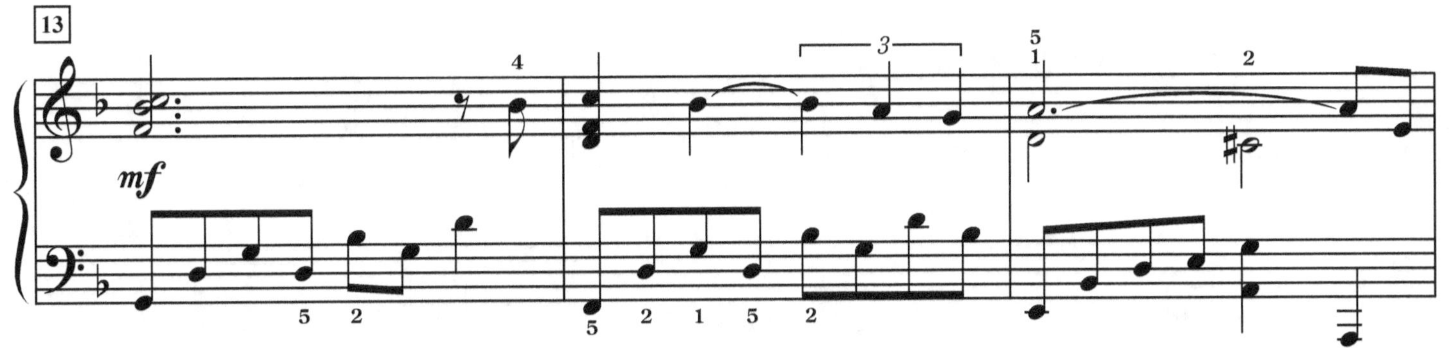
13
mf

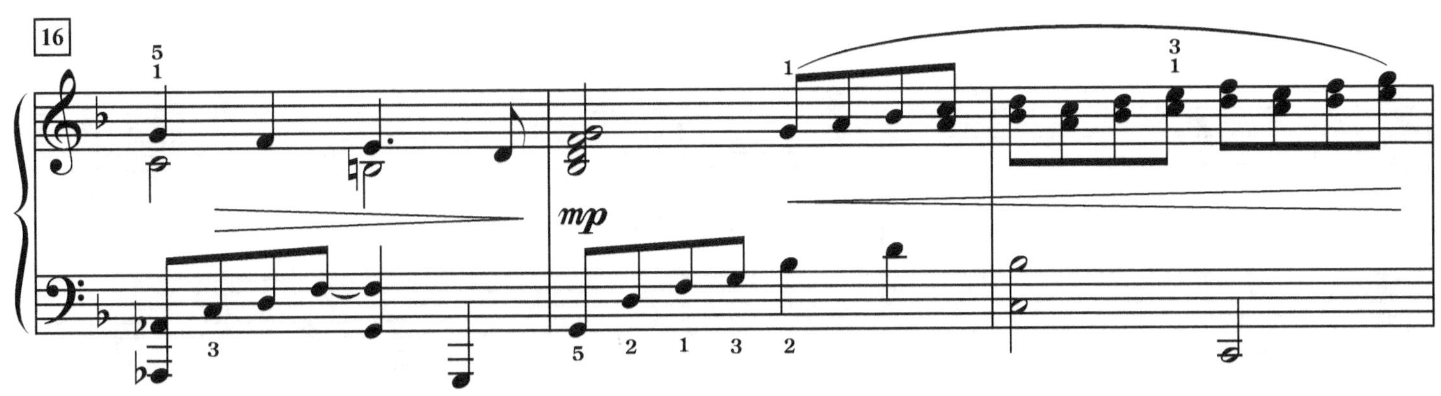
16
mp

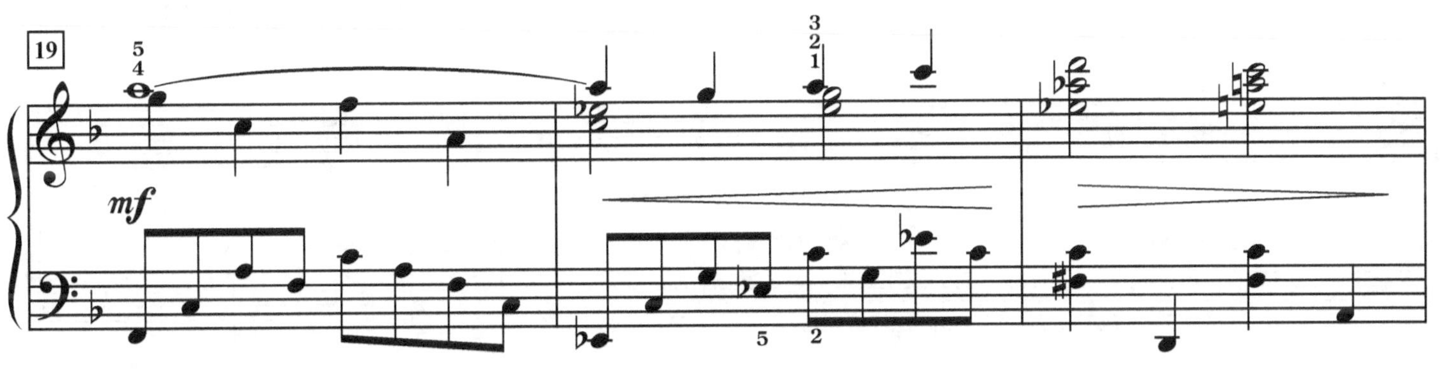
19
mf

22

26

29
f
mf

32
1.
mp

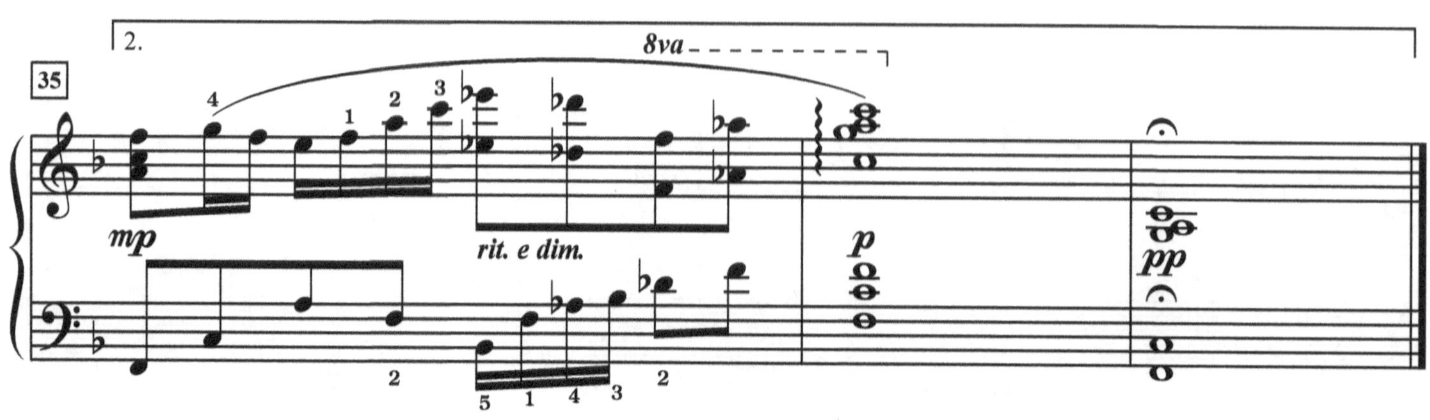
2.
35
8va
mp
rit. e dim.
p
pp

Endless Love
(from *Endless Love*)

Words and Music by Lionel Richie
Arranged by Dan Coates

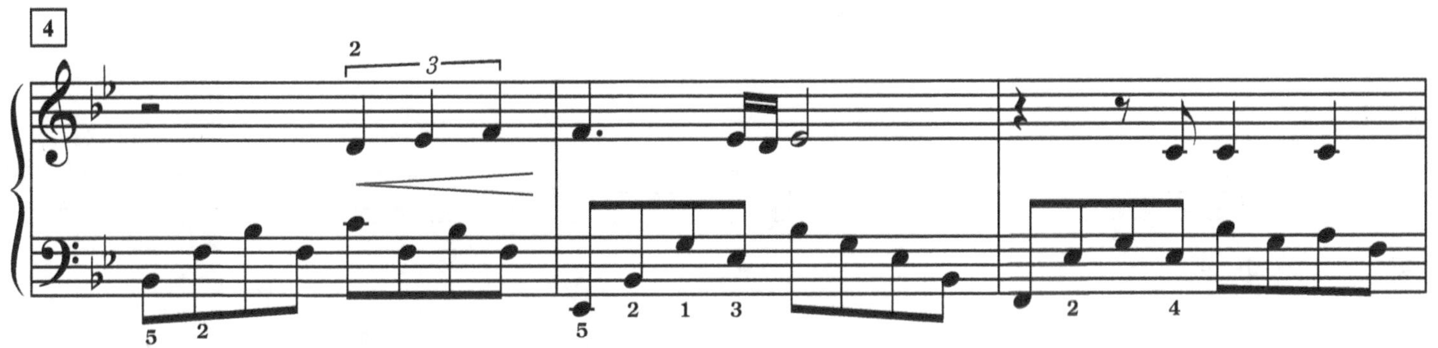

mf
f

28
8va
dim.
mp
31
1.
34
2.
37
40
mf

43
cresc.
46
f
49
52
55
f

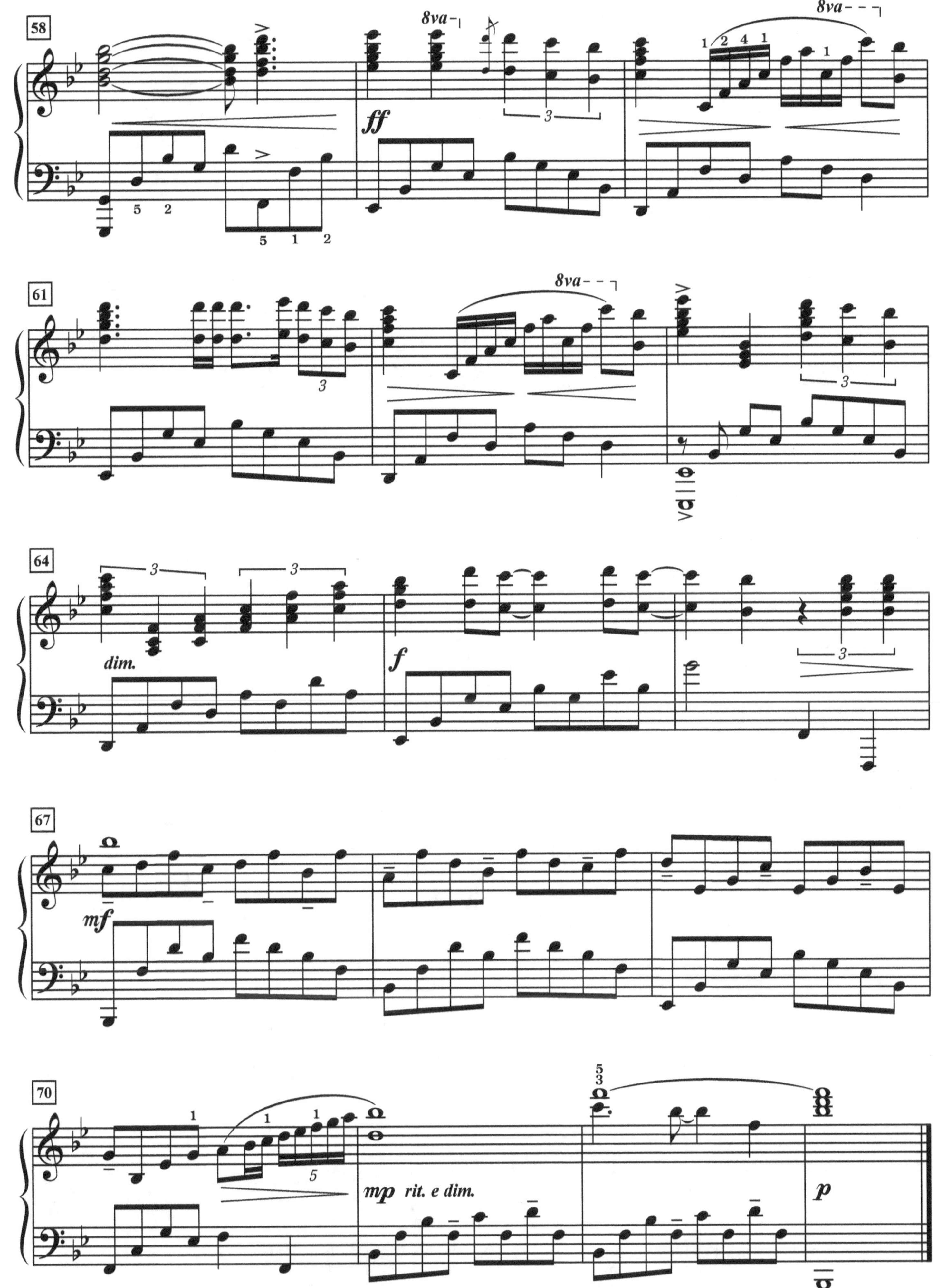
58
8va
ff
61
64
dim.
f
67
mf
70
mp rit. e dim.
p

Miss Celie's Blues
(from *The Color Purple*)

Words by Quincy Jones, Rod Temperton and Lionel Richie
Music by Quincy Jones and Rod Temperton
Arranged by Dan Coates

Movie Solos

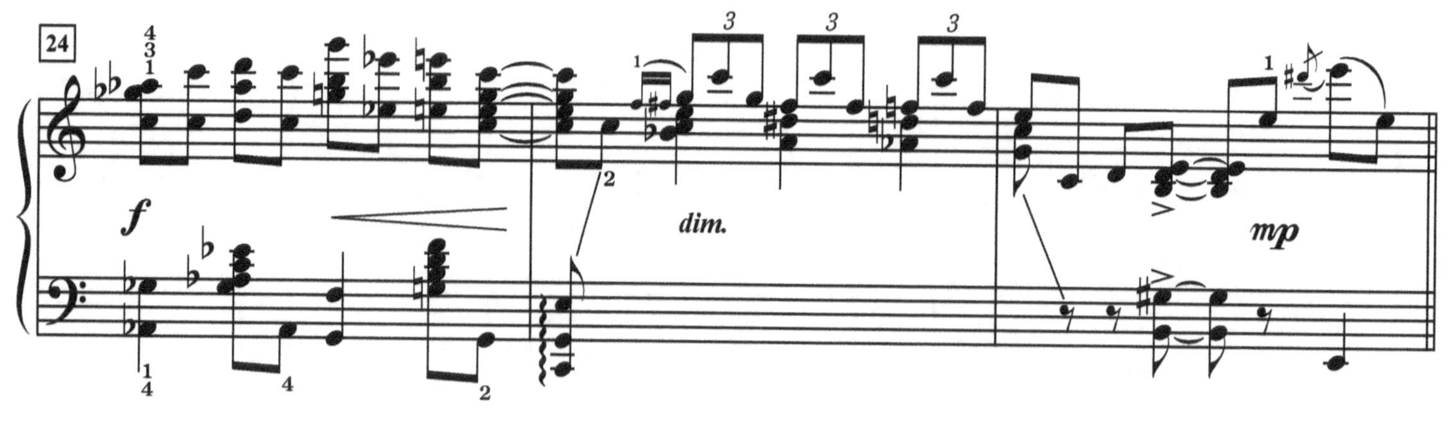
24
f
dim.
mp

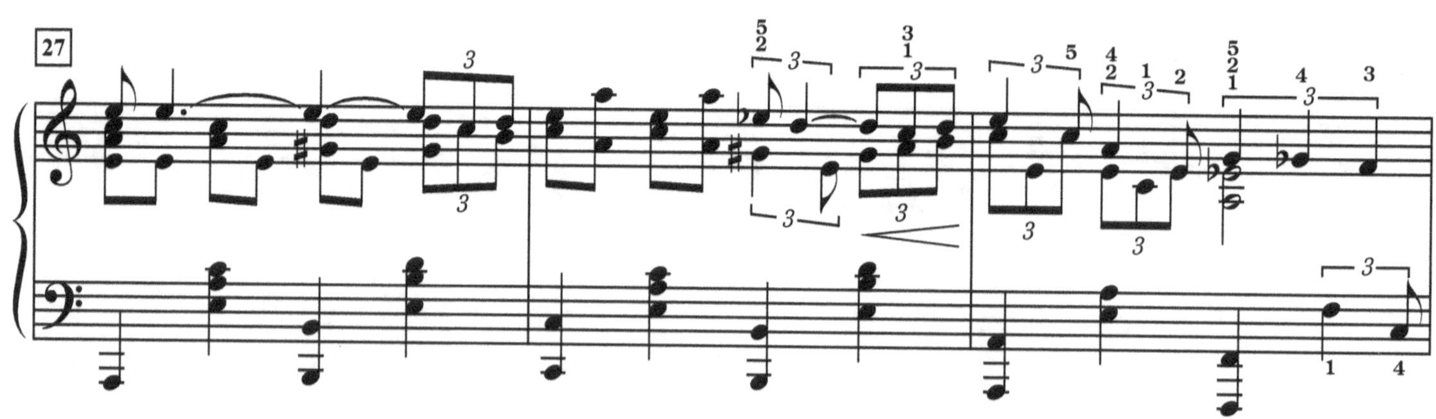
27

30
8va
mf

33
cresc.

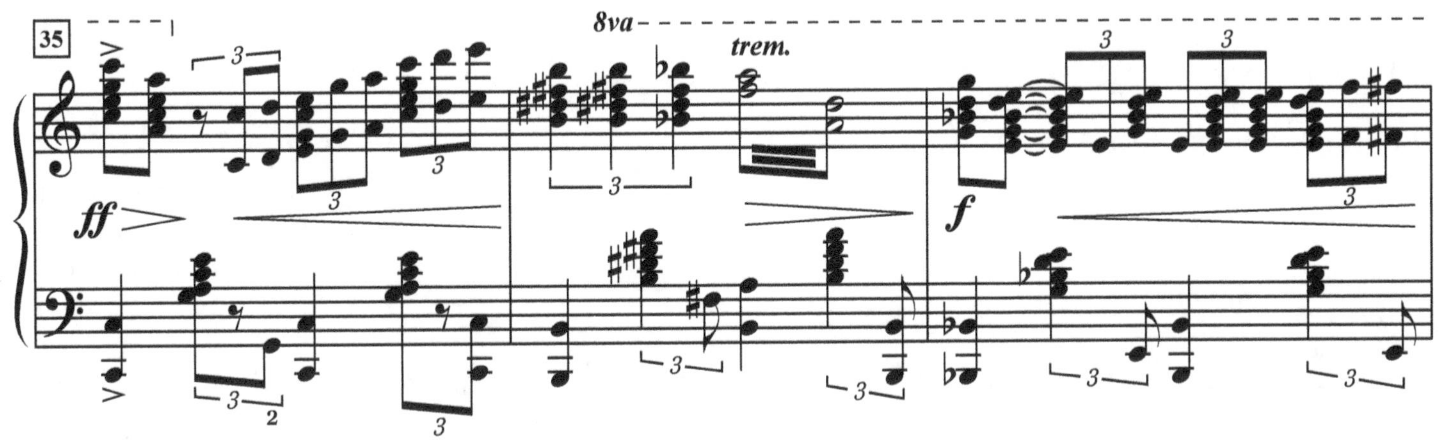
35
8va
trem.
ff
f

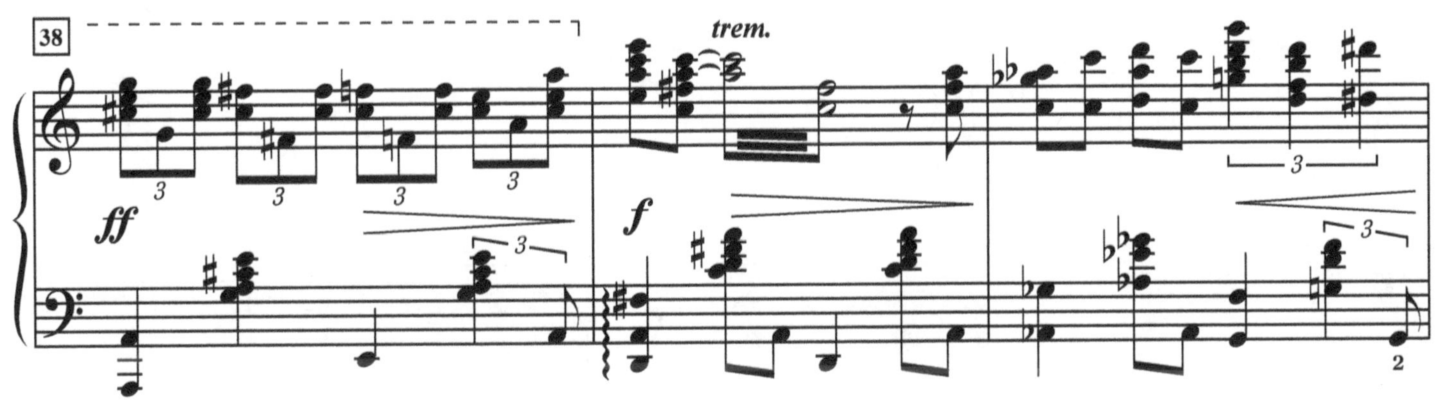
38
trem.
ff
f

41
f
sfz
mf

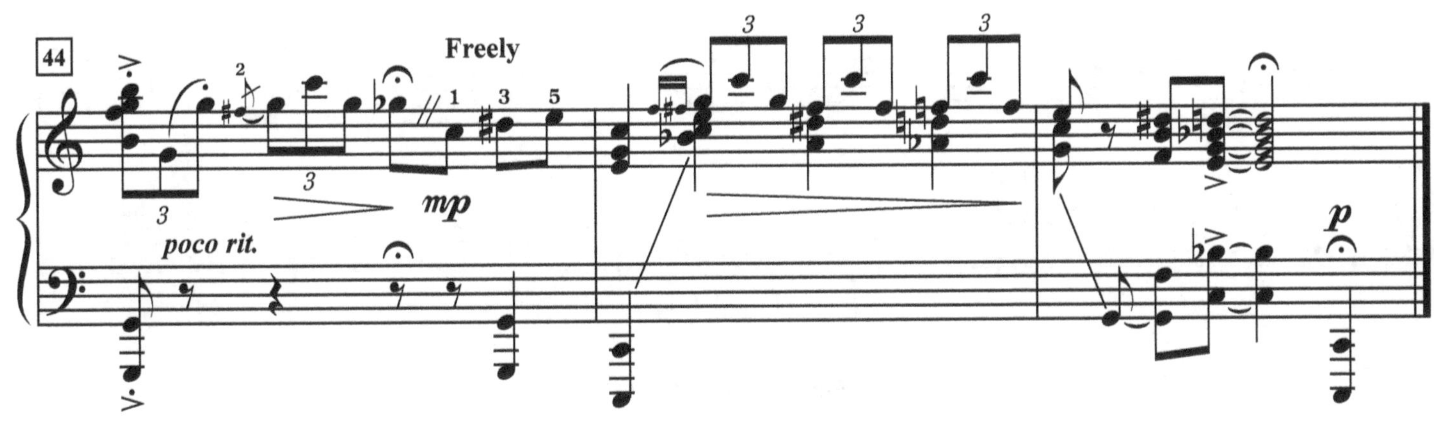
44
Freely
mp
poco rit.
p

Hooray for Hollywood
(from *The Hollywood Hotel*)

Words by Johnny Mercer
Music by Richard A. Whiting
Arranged by Dan Coates

17
21
f
pedal ad lib.
25
cresc.
ff
29
mf
33

37
f
41
3
5
45
49
ff
1.
2.
53
3
3

The Notebook (Main Title)
(from *The Notebook*)

Written by Aaron Zigman
Arranged by Dan Coates

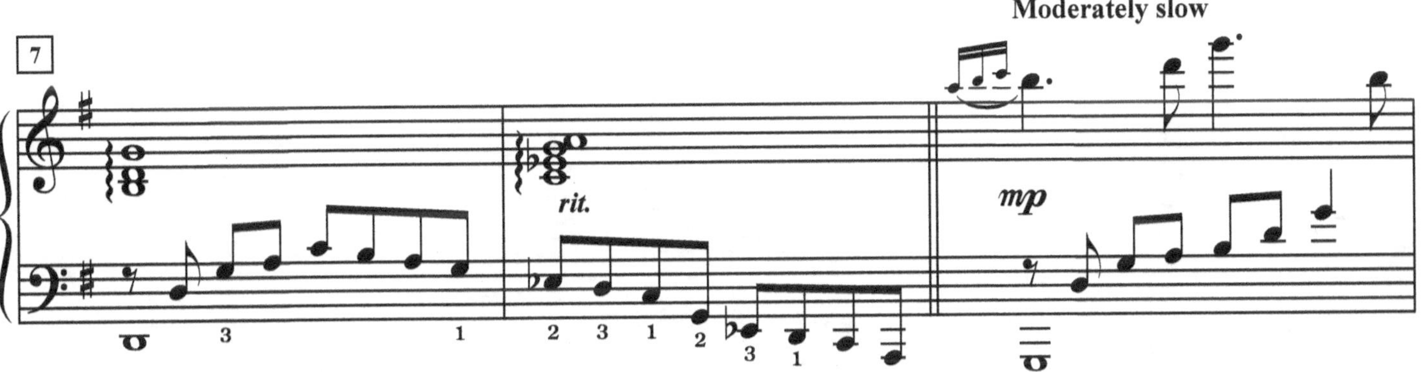

Movie Solos

13
Slower
mf
rit.
16
Faster, moving ahead
mp
rit.
mf
19
cresc.
f
22
25
mf molto rit.

Moderately slow
27
mp
mf
30
f
33
mf
1 2 3
35
mp rit. poco a poco
3
3
Tempo I
8va
p
38
rit.
pp

Over the Rainbow
(from *The Wizard of Oz*)

Music by Harold Arlen
Lyrics by E.Y. Harburg
Arranged by Dan Coates

Movie Solos

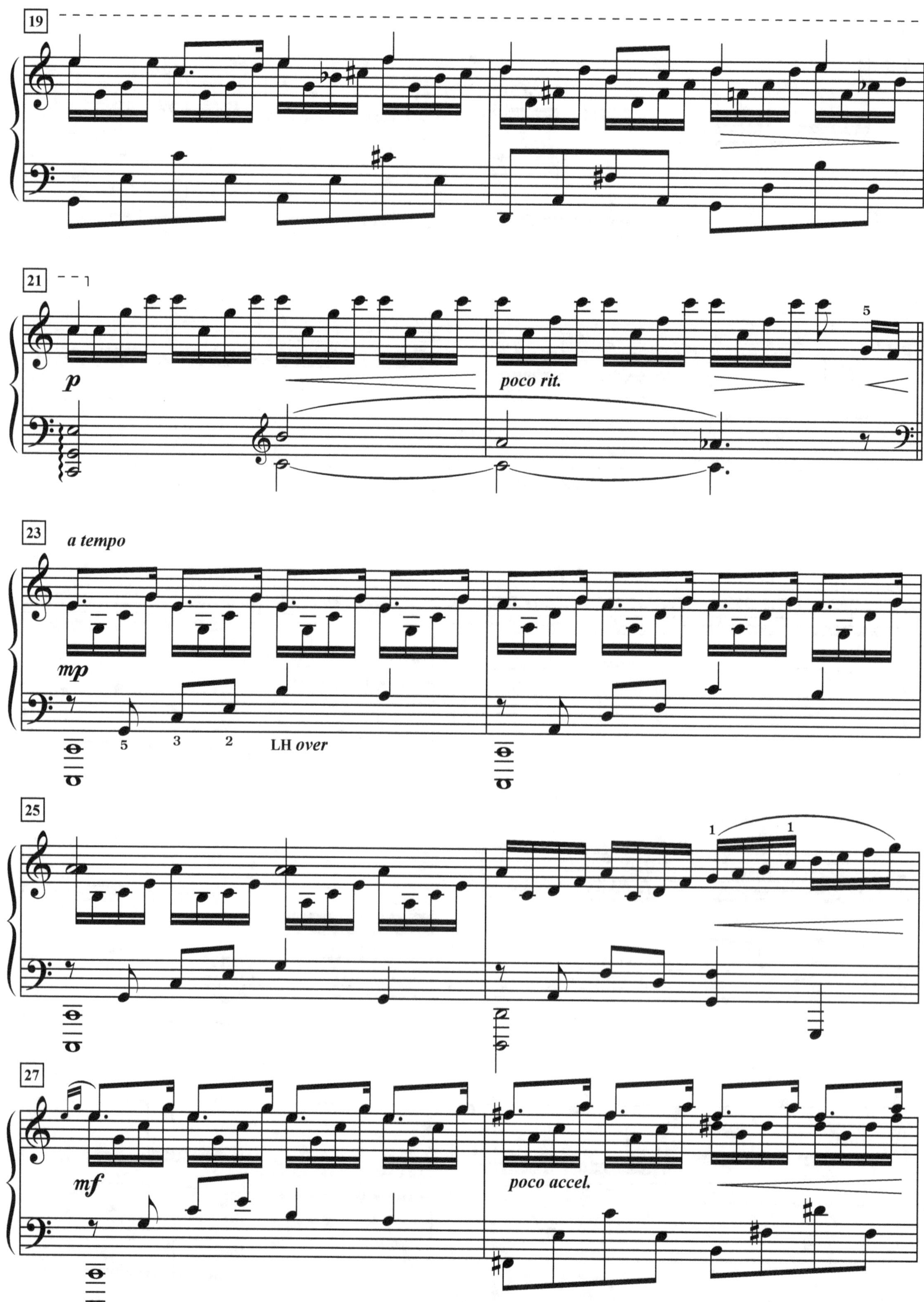
19
21
p
poco rit.
5
23
a tempo
mp
5
3
2
LH over
25
1
1
27
mf
poco accel.

Più mosso

29

f *rit.*

Tempo I

31

8va *ff*

33

8va *f*

35

mf *dim.*

37

Slower

poco rit. *p* LH

39
mp
41
43
8va
f
45
Meno mosso
Tempo I
mf rit.
mp
p
48
rit.
Very slowly
8va
(both hands)
pp
ppp

Theme from *New York, New York*
(from *New York, New York*)

Music by John Kander
Words by Fred Ebb
Arranged by Dan Coates

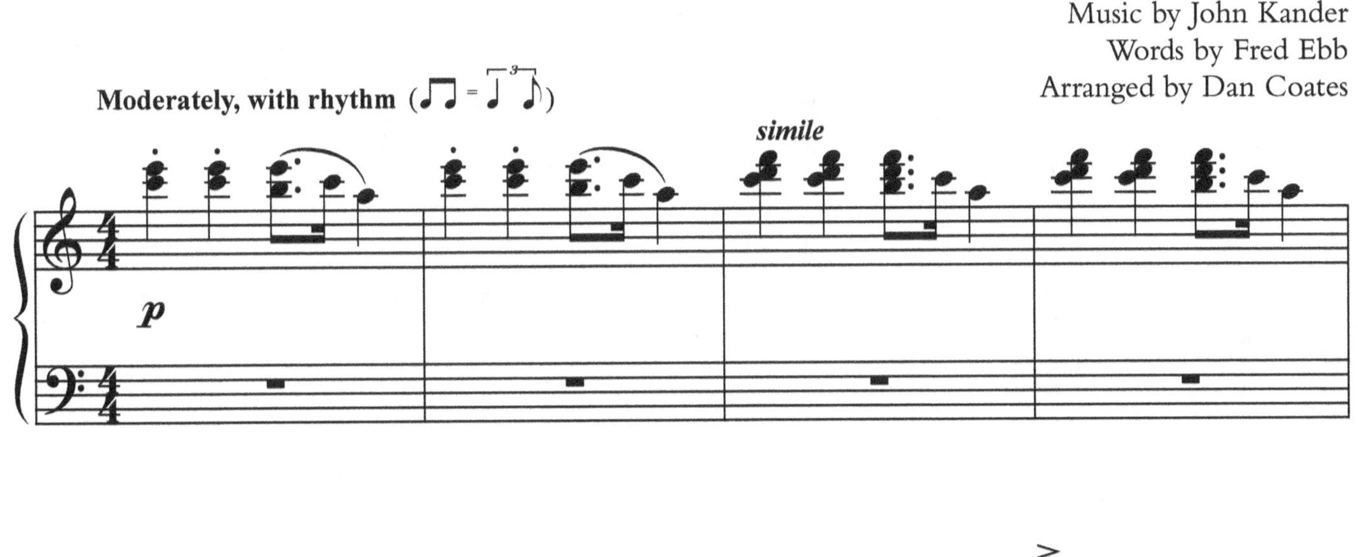

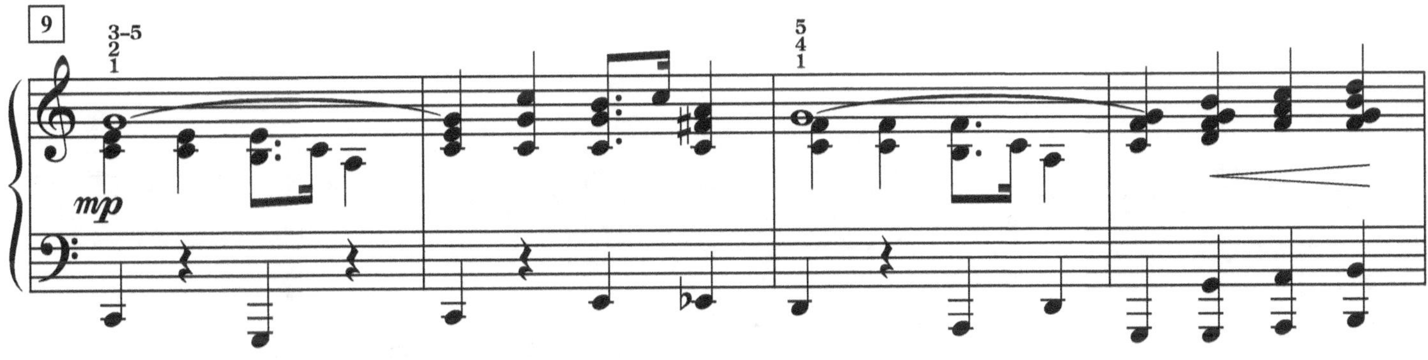

Movie Solos

16
f
3
mf
19
3
5
3
2
3
3
3
3
f
22
8va
3
1
2
3
4
1
2
3
1
2
mp
3
3
3
f
3
3
25
mf
3
5
3
2
5
4
2
4
1
28
3
f
3

8va
31
mp
sfz
mf
34
8va
f
37
mf
40
f
43
mf
f

47
sfz
mp
cresc.
51
f
mp
54
8va
f
mf
57
f
61
Meno mosso
molto rit.

64
Slower
ff
8va
68
f
71
sfz
ff
74
f
mf
f sustained
78
ff
sub. mp
ff
sfz

That's Entertainment!
(from *The Band Wagon*)

Words by Howard Dietz
Music by Arthur Schwartz
Arranged by Dan Coates

Brightly, with spirit

f

pedal lightly

5

mf

9

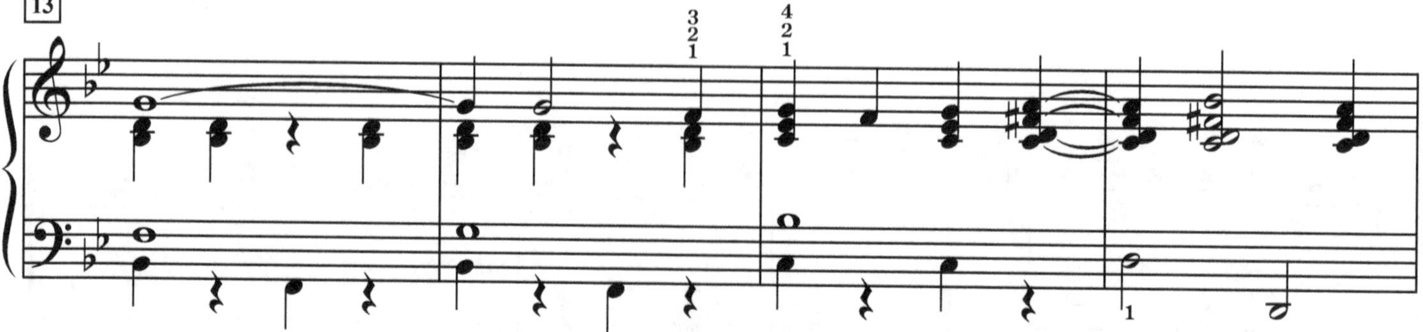

17
4
2
1
1
2
3
1
3
5
21
3
1
f
25
mf
29
1
33
1
2
3
1
2
3
5

37
f
5
41
4
2
1
5
4
2
mf
45
5
1
3
2
f
49
2
1
5
2
1
mf
53
f
3
1

57
mf
61
cresc. poco a poco
65
f
ff
70
75
1.
2.
f
mf
f
sfz

The Windmills of Your Mind
(from *The Thomas Crowne Affair*)

Words by Alan and Marilyn Bergman
Music by Michel Legrand
Arranged by Dan Coates

15
rit.
19
a tempo
mp
23
mf
27
30
rit.

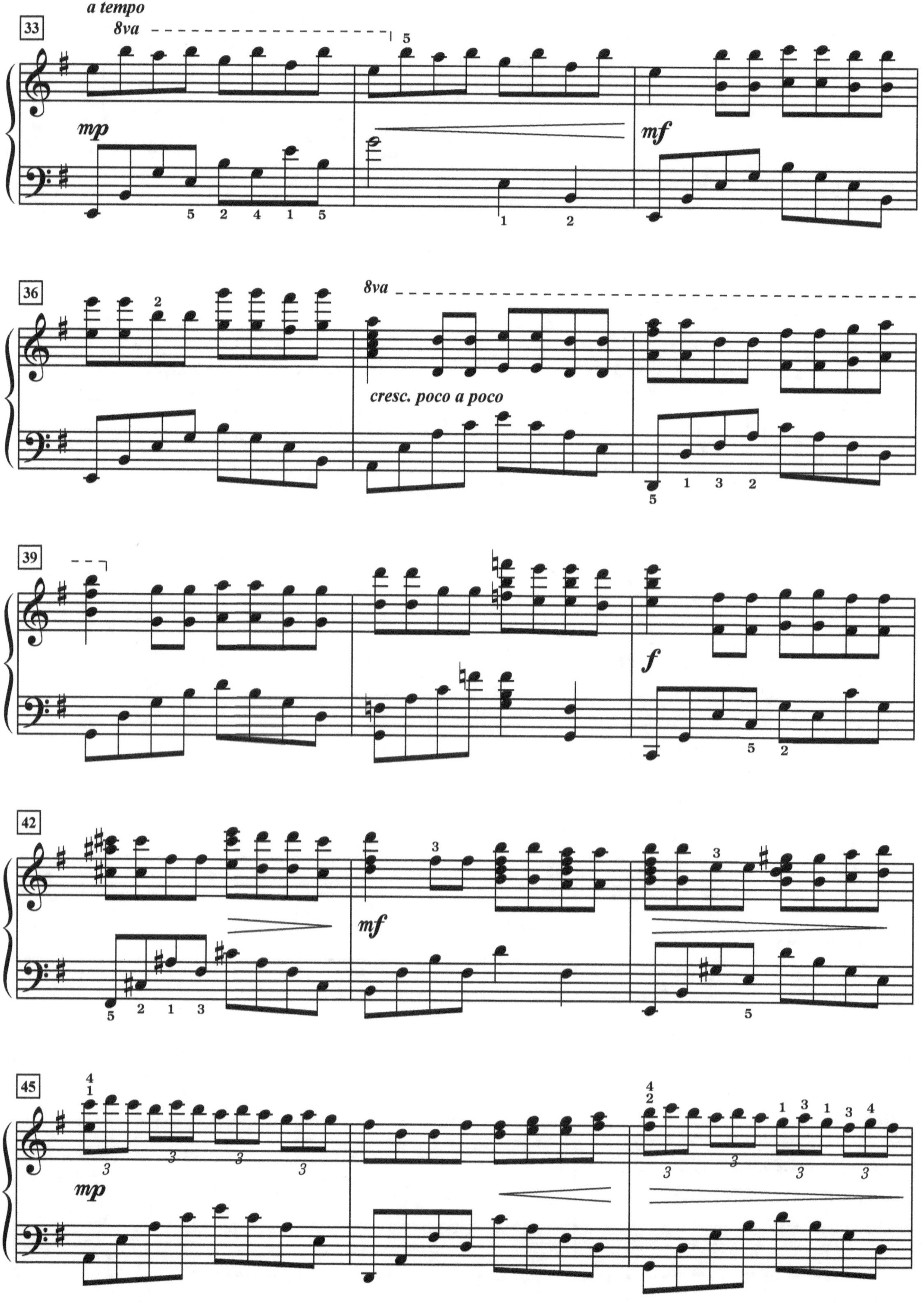
33
a tempo
8va
mp
mf
36
8va
cresc. poco a poco
39
f
42
mf
45
mp

48
rit.
51
a tempo
p
54
mp
57
poco rit.
Slower
60
8va
p
rit.
pp

The Wind Beneath My Wings
(from *Beaches*)

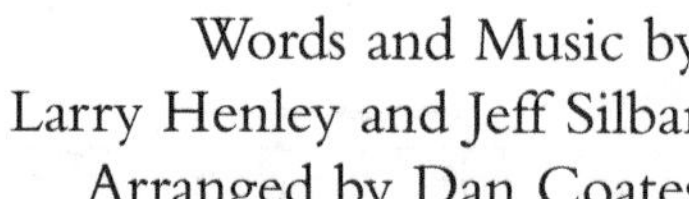

Words and Music by
Larry Henley and Jeff Silbar
Arranged by Dan Coates

Moderately

mp legato

with pedal

simile

4

rit.

a tempo

mp

7

11

mf

15
18
1.
rit.
2., 3.
21
f
24
27
mf

30

f

34

dim.

mf

to Coda

37

mp

rit.

D.S. al Coda

Coda

mp

44

rit.

a tempo

p

8va

rit.

pp

This page is intentionally left blank to avoid awkward page turns.

Can You Feel the Love Tonight
(from *The Lion King*)

Music by Elton John
Words by Tim Rice
Arranged by Dan Coates

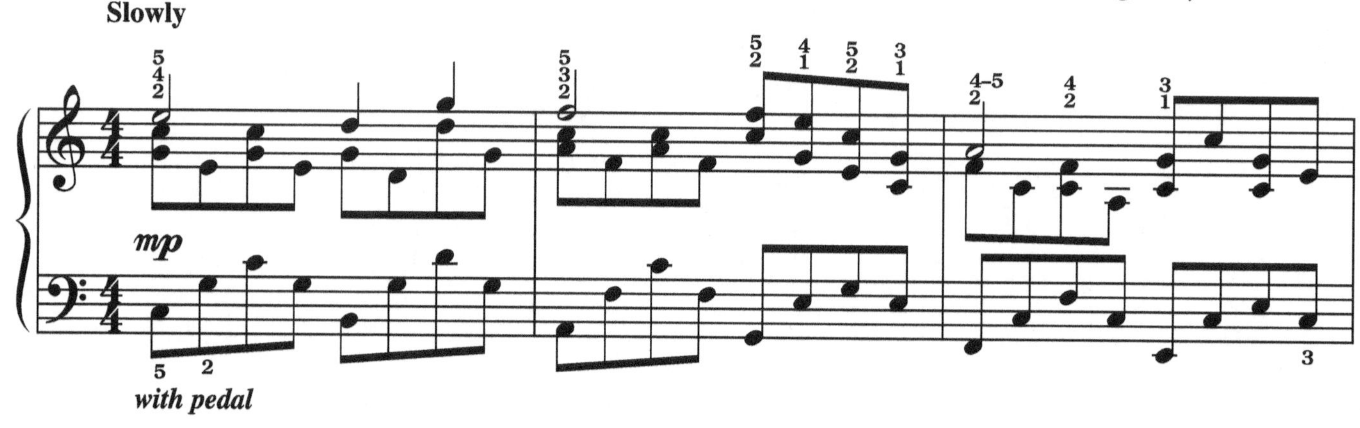

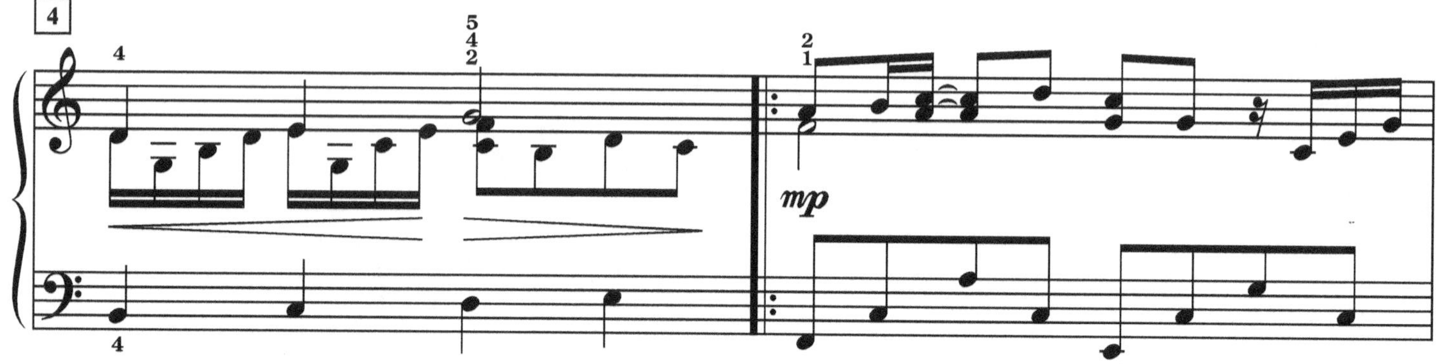

10
5
2
5
1
3

1.
To measure 15
2.
12
5
5

14
1
15
5
4
2
mf
5
2
5
1
4

17
5
4
2
4
2
3
5
4
5

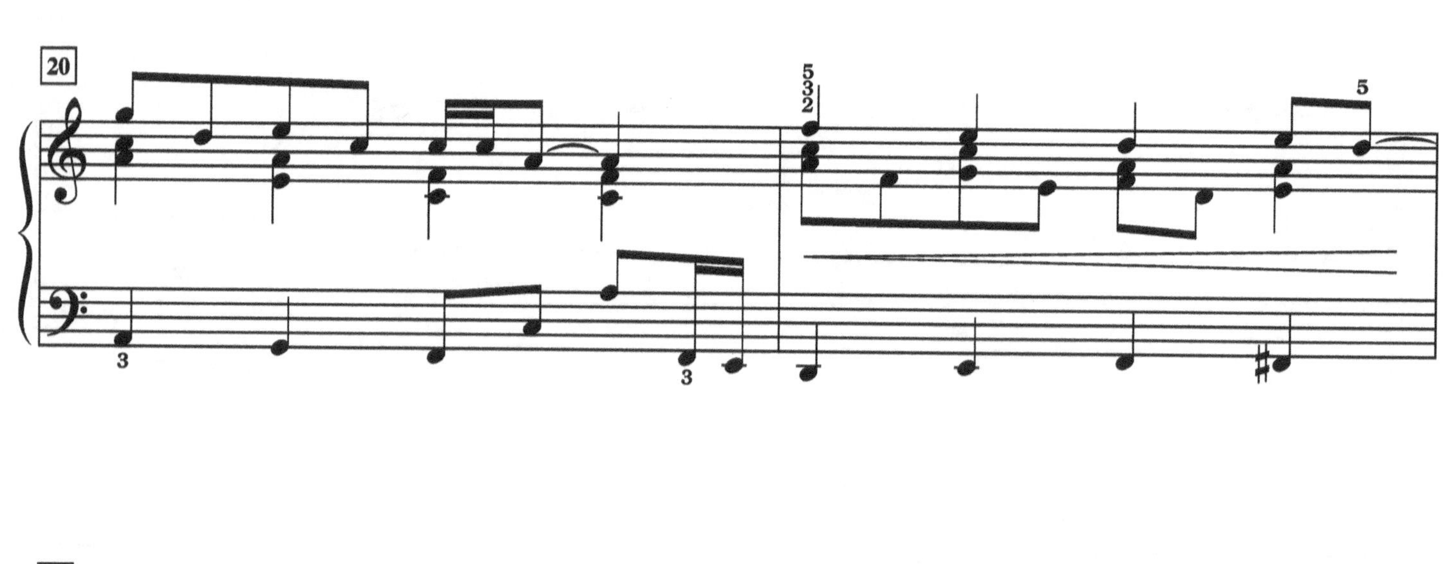
20

22
mf

24

26

28
f

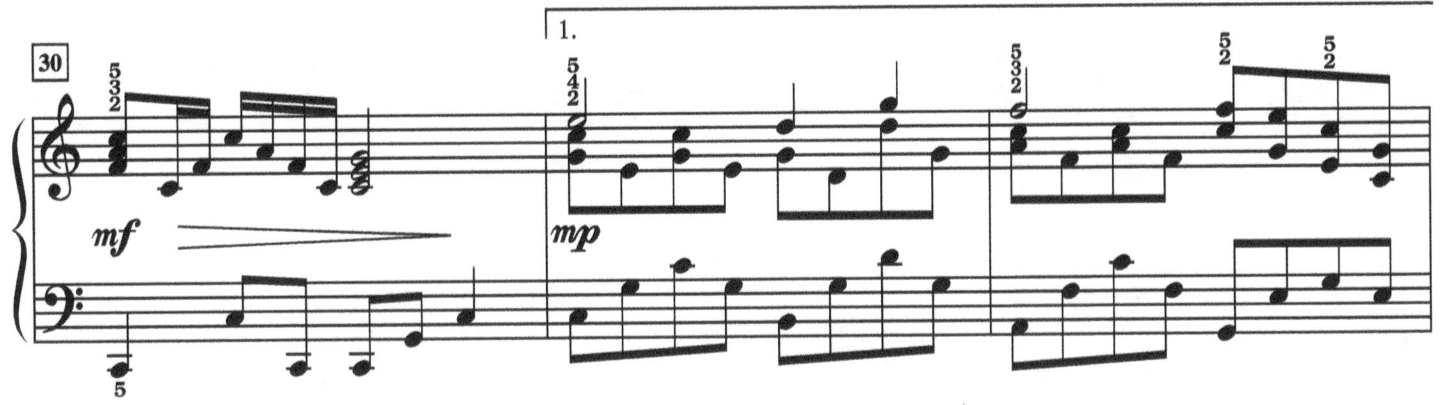
30
1.
mf
mp

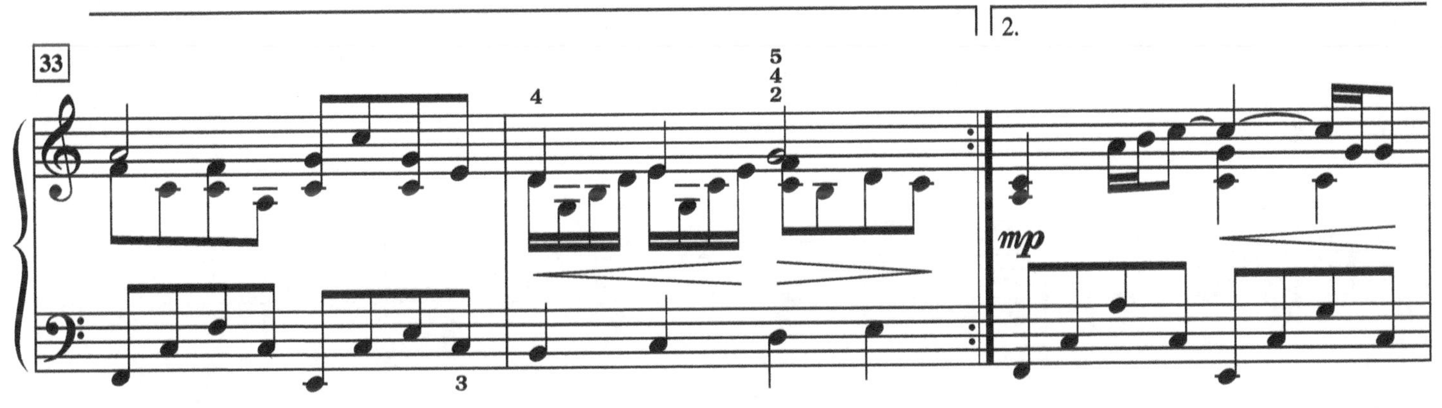
33
2.
mp

36
rit.
molto rit.

Everything's Coming Up Roses
(from *Gypsy*)

Lyrics by Stephen Sondheim
Music by Jule Styne
Arranged by Dan Coates

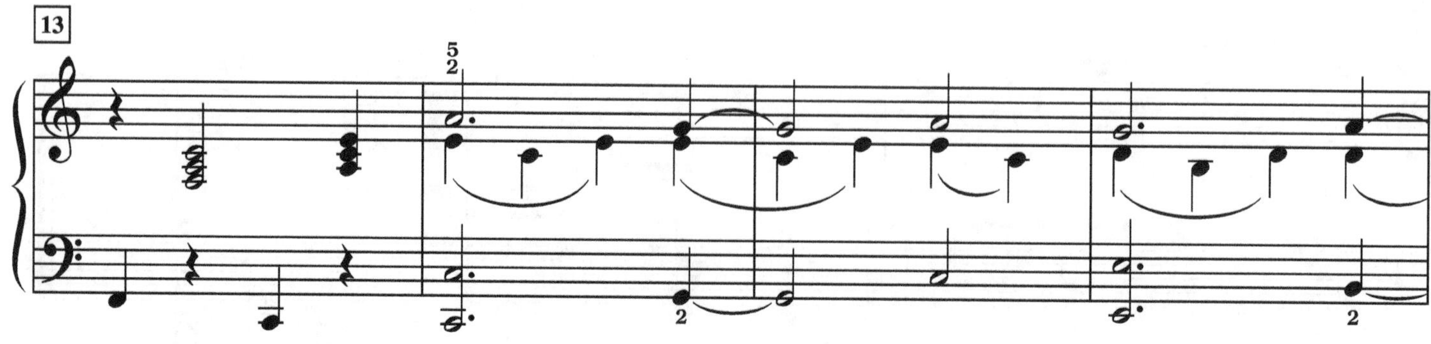

17
21
f
25
29
mf
33
f

37
41
mf
45
49
53
cresc.
f

57
2
1
61
2
1
65
mf
69
73
5
mp cresc. poco a poco
5

77
f
81
85
89
1.
94
2.
mf

98

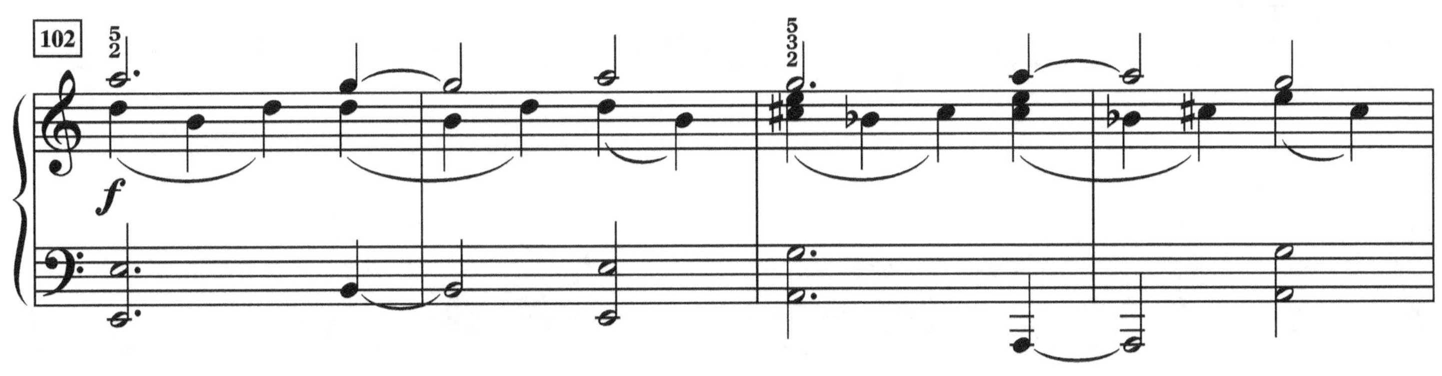
102
f

106
cresc.

110
ff
f

HOME
(FROM *THE WIZ*)

Words and Music by Charlie Smalls
Arranged by Dan Coates

5
mp
with pedal

8
simile

11

14

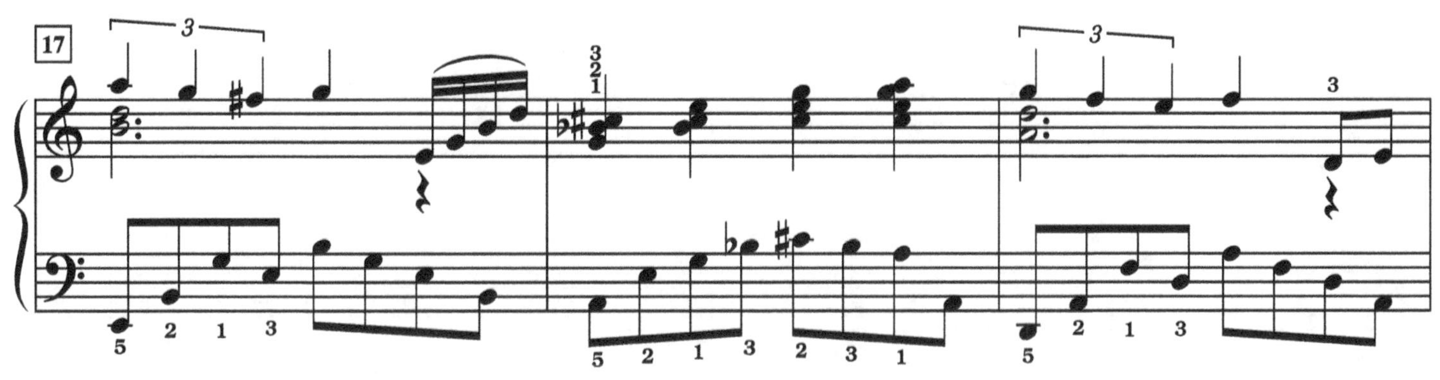
17

20
mp

23

26

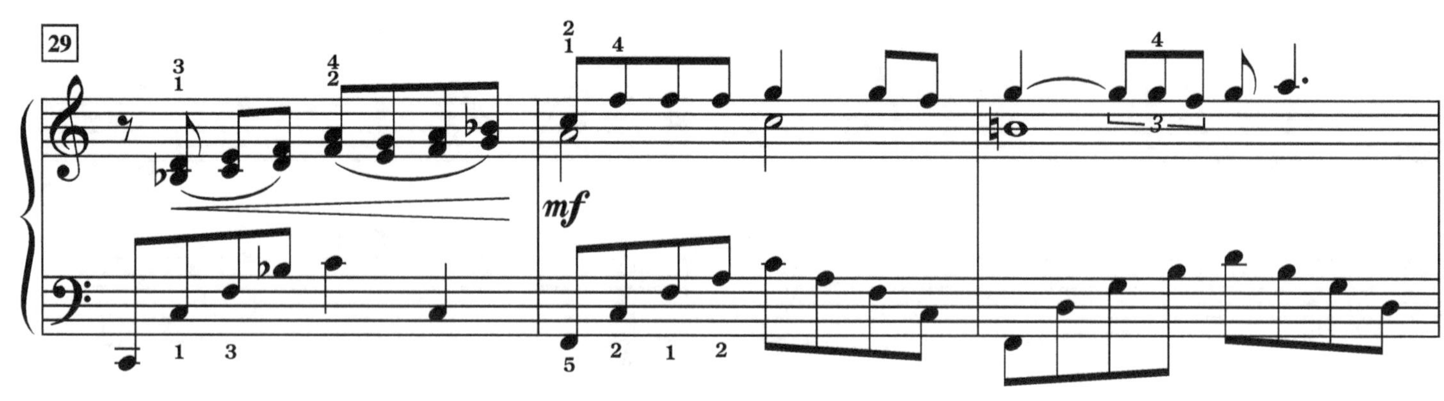
29
mf

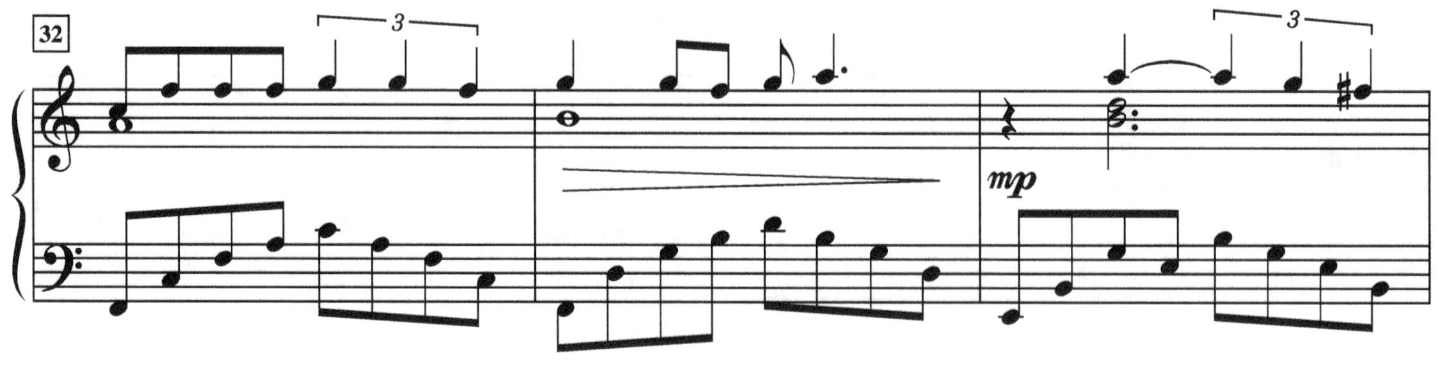
32
mp

35

38
mp

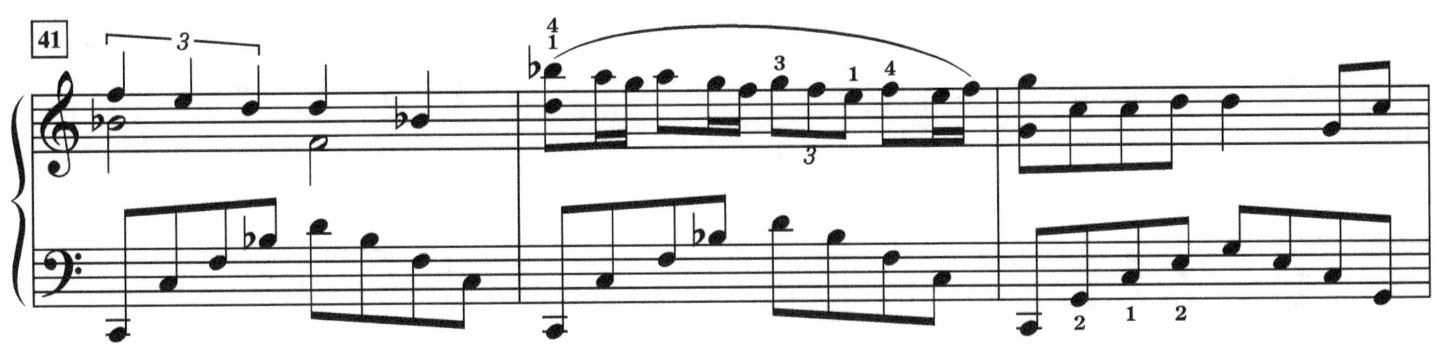
41

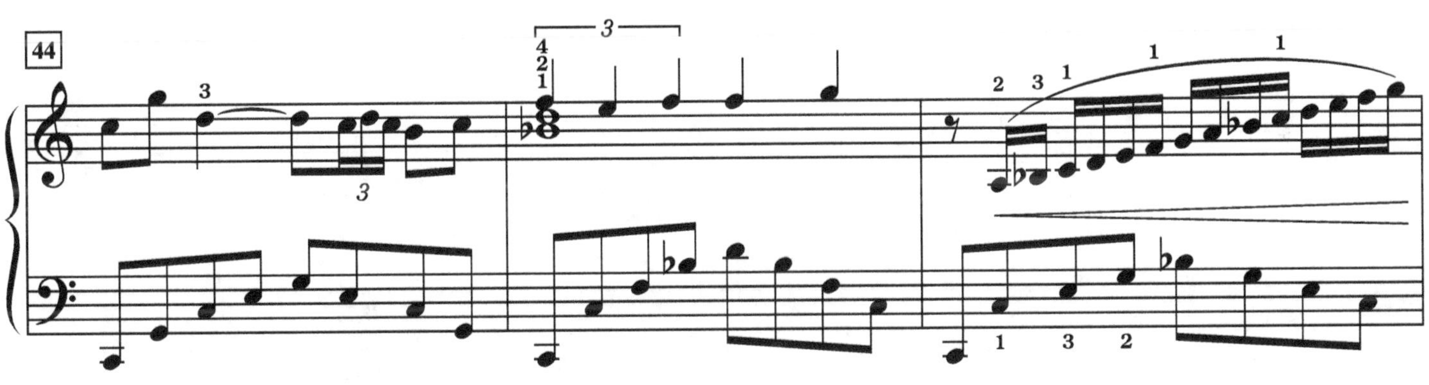
44

47
mf

62
3
3
ff

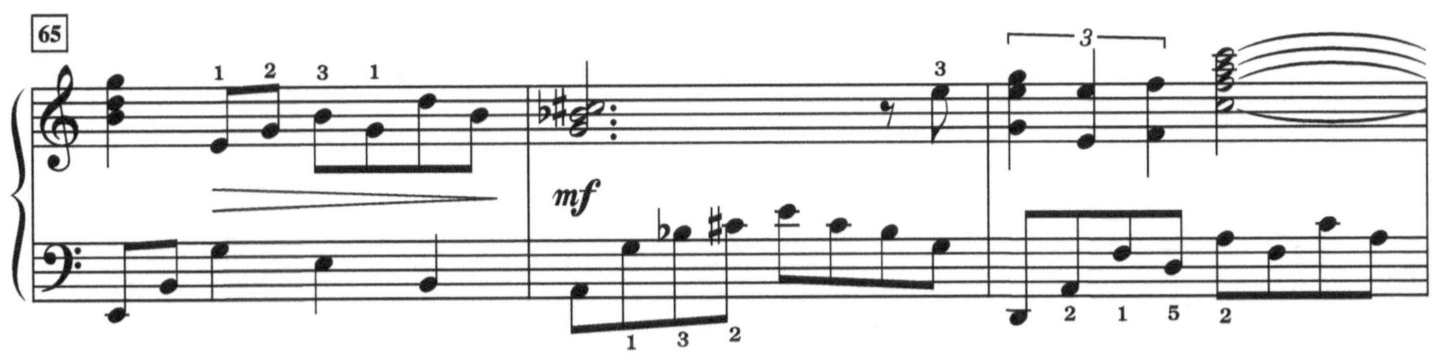
65
mf

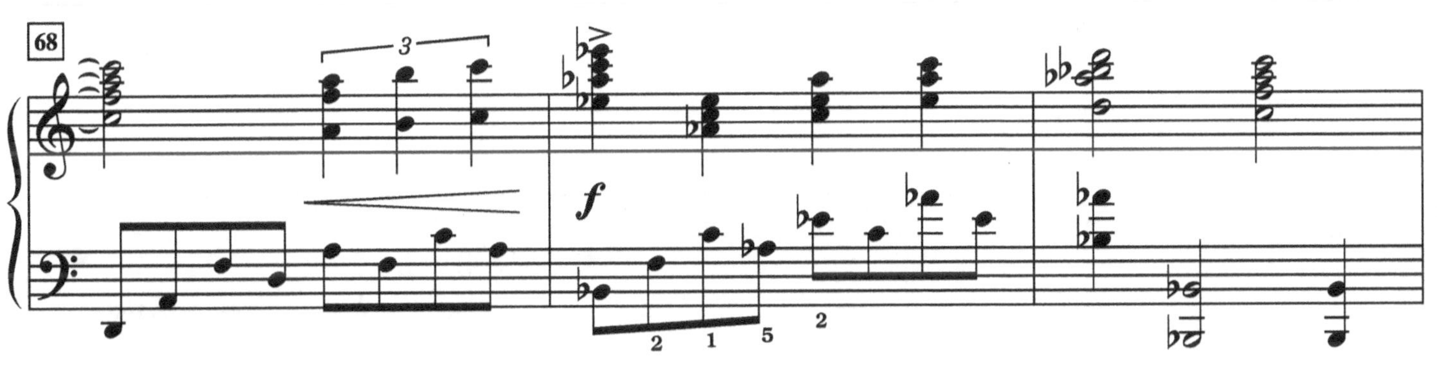
68
3
f

71
mf
molto cresc.
fff
rit.

I Could Have Danced All Night
(from *My Fair Lady*)

Lyrics by Alan Jay Lerner
Music by Frederick Loewe
Arranged by Dan Coates

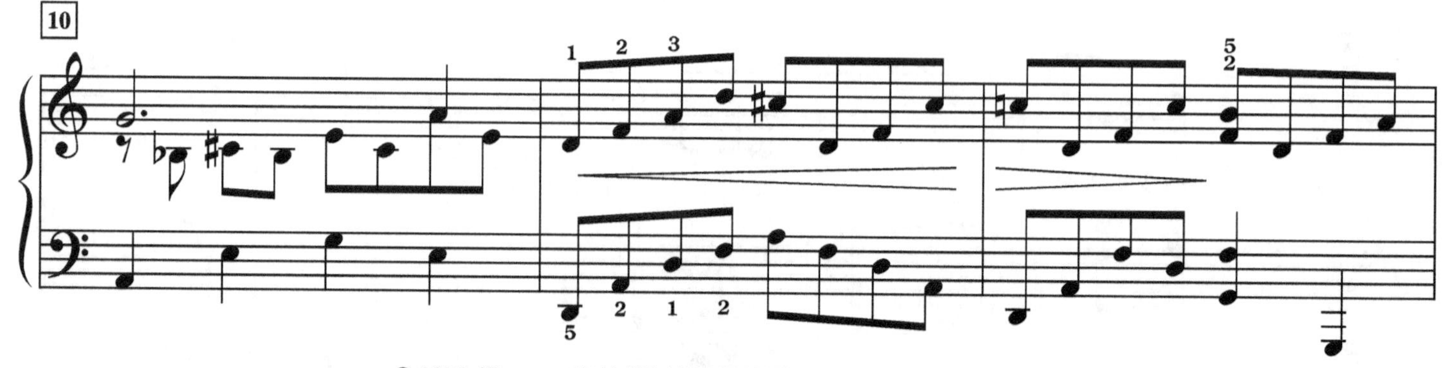

Broadway Hits

25

28
f

31

34
mp
mf

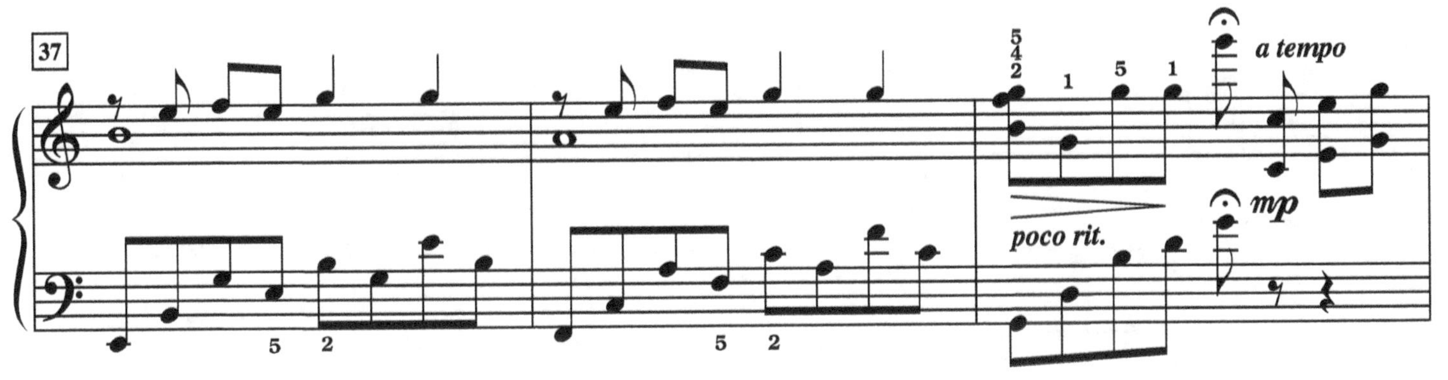
37
a tempo
mp
poco rit.

40

43

46

49

52
5
4
2

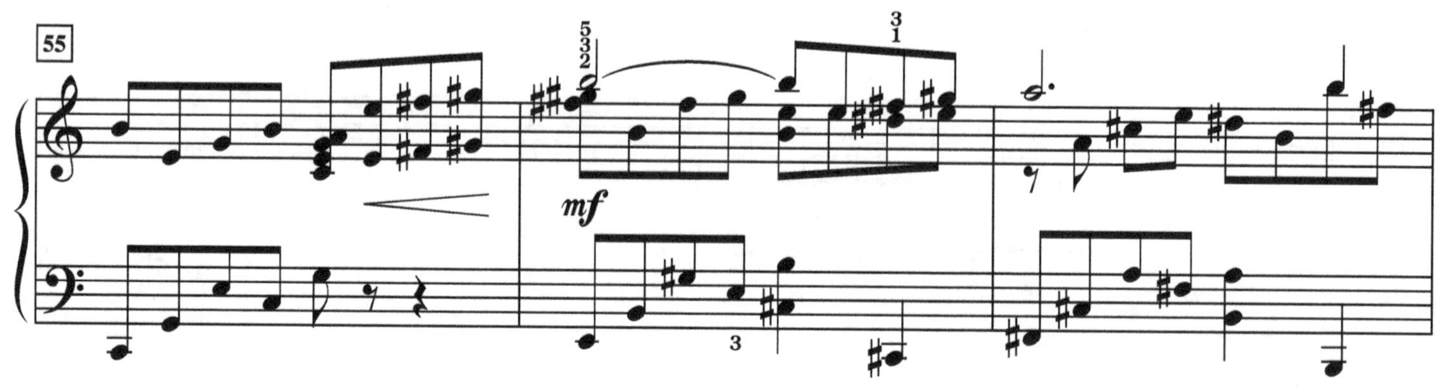
55
5
3
2
mf
3
1
3

58
5
4
f

61
meno mosso
ff

a tempo
64
f

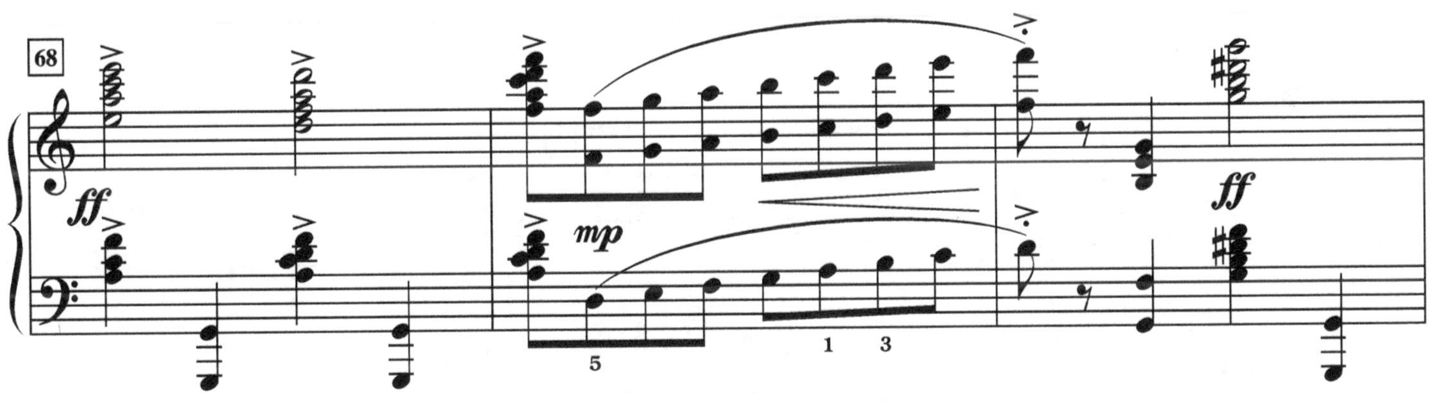
68
ff
mp
ff

71
mf
f
8va
ff

Lily's Eyes
(from *The Secret Garden*)

Lyrics by Marsha Norman
Music by Lucy Simon
Arranged by Dan Coates

12
5
4
2
3
1
3
2
1
3
(4)
2

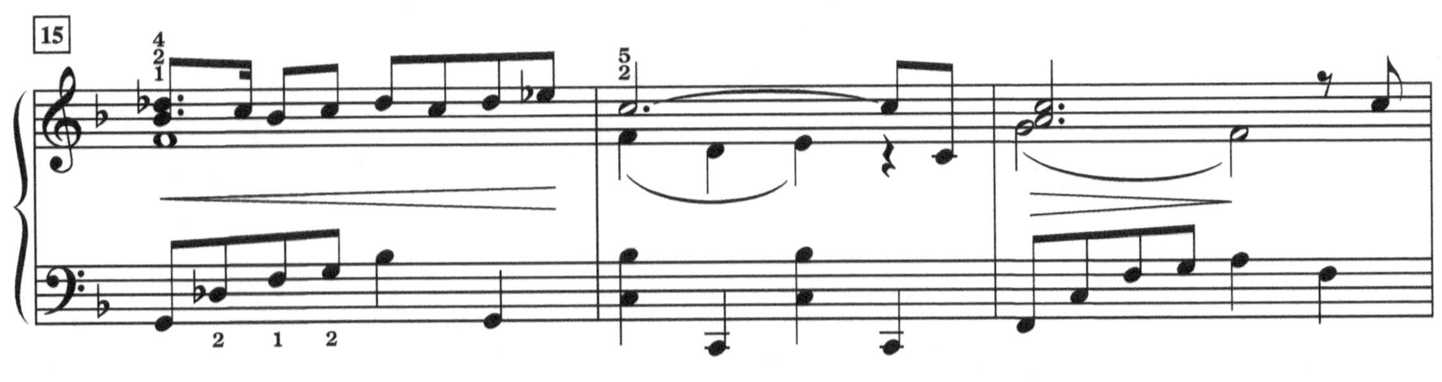
15
4
2
1
5
2
2
1
2

18
5
mp

21
8va
mf
5
2

24
f
27
30
33
mf
36
cresc.
8va
rit.

Broadway Hits

Look to the Rainbow

(from *Finian's Rainbow*)

Words by E.Y. Harburg
Music by Burton Lane
Arranged by Dan Coates

Moderately slow, freely

17
mf
21
25
29
mp rit.
33 a tempo

37
5
5
5
41
2
5
2
2
cresc.
45
mf
2
3
1
mp
1
2
49
2
mf
5
53

57
5
5
61
3
1
4
2
mp
3
65
69
mf
rit.
2
1
4
72
a tempo
8va
mp
p

IF EVER I WOULD LEAVE YOU

(FROM *CAMELOT*)

Music by Frederick Loewe
Lyrics by Alan Jay Lerner
Arranged by Dan Coates

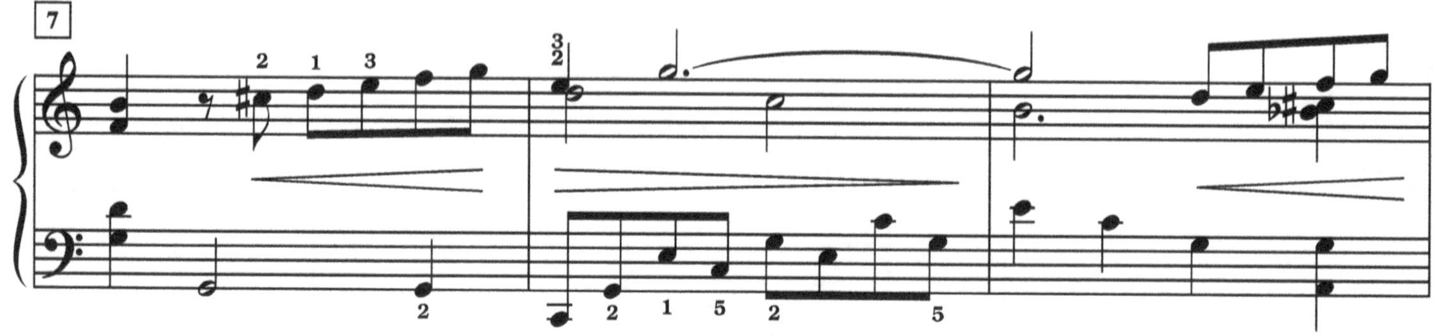

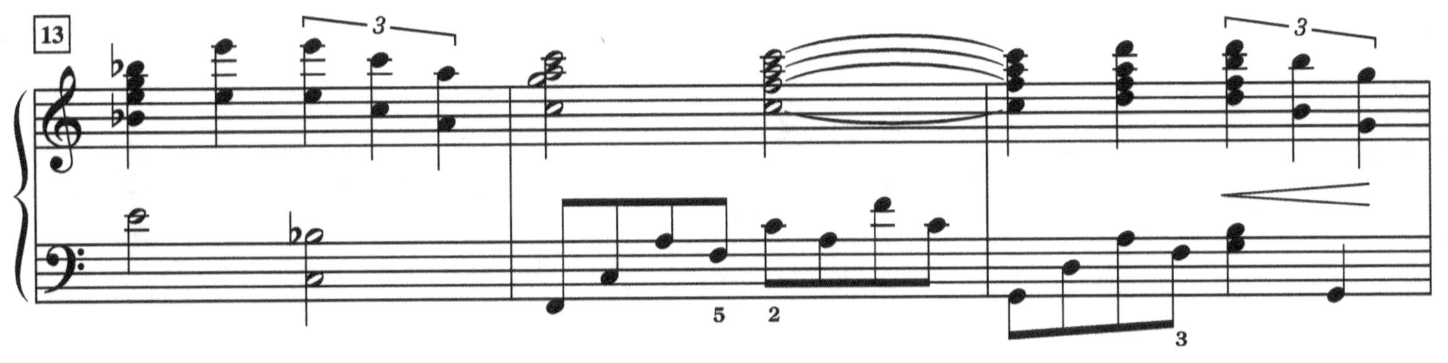
13
3
3

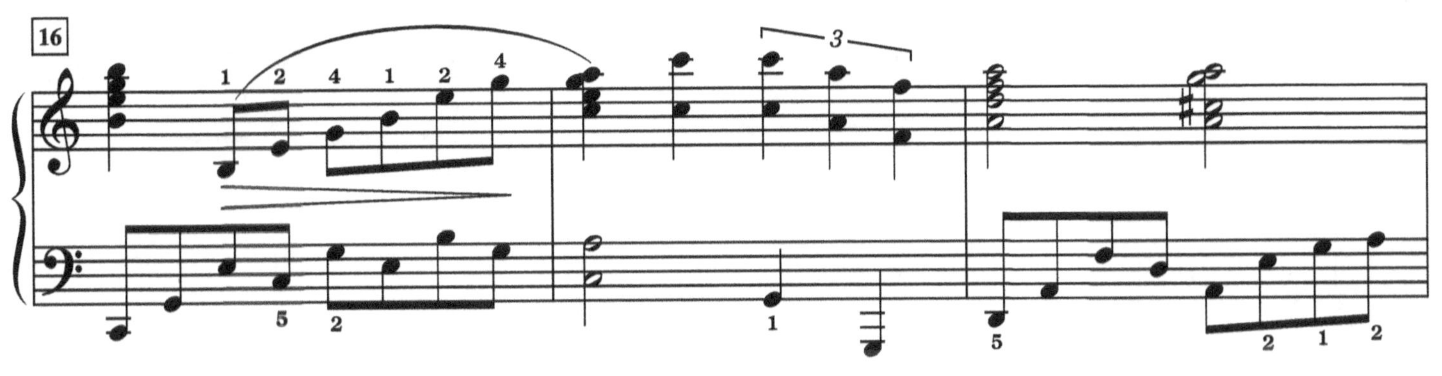
16
3

19
dim.
mp
3

22

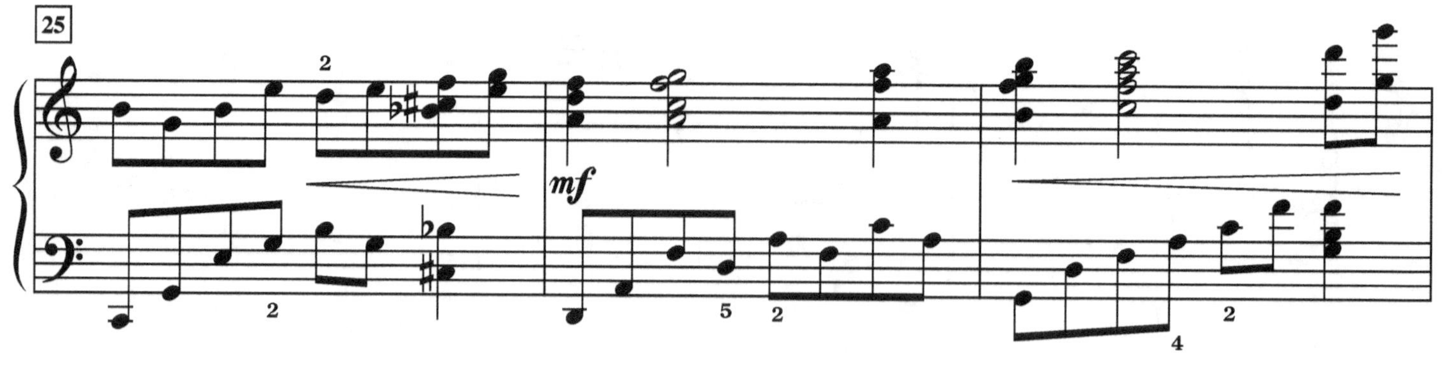
25
mf

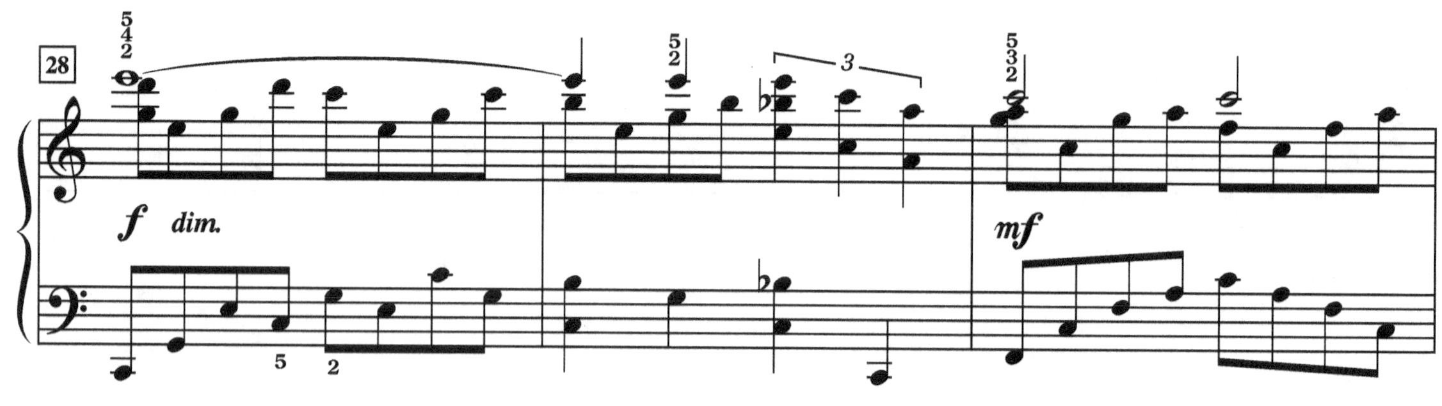
28
f dim.
mf

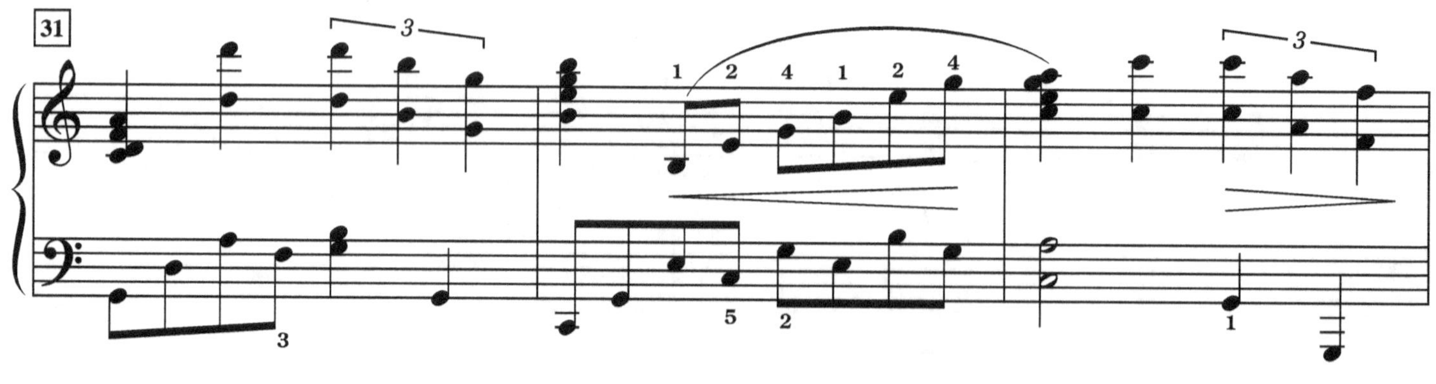
31

34

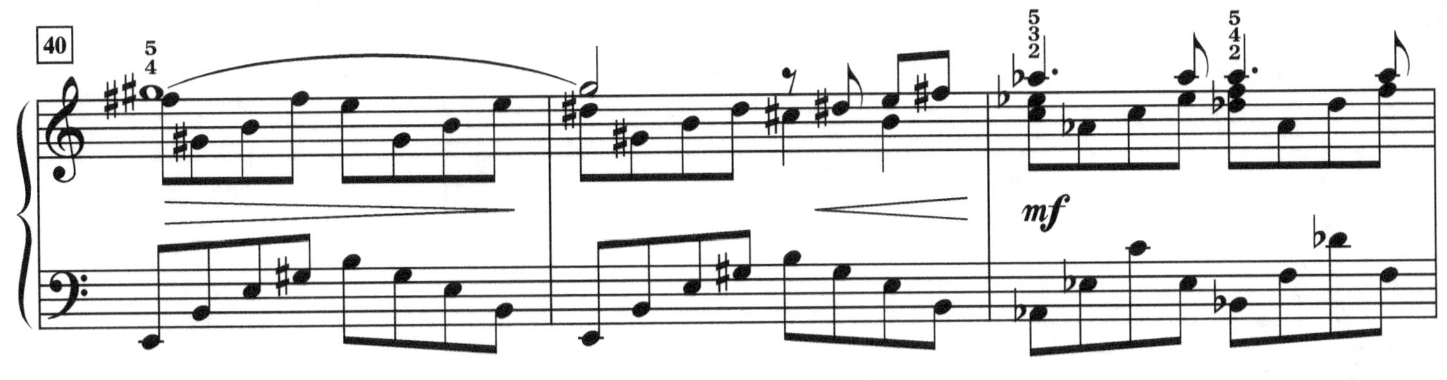

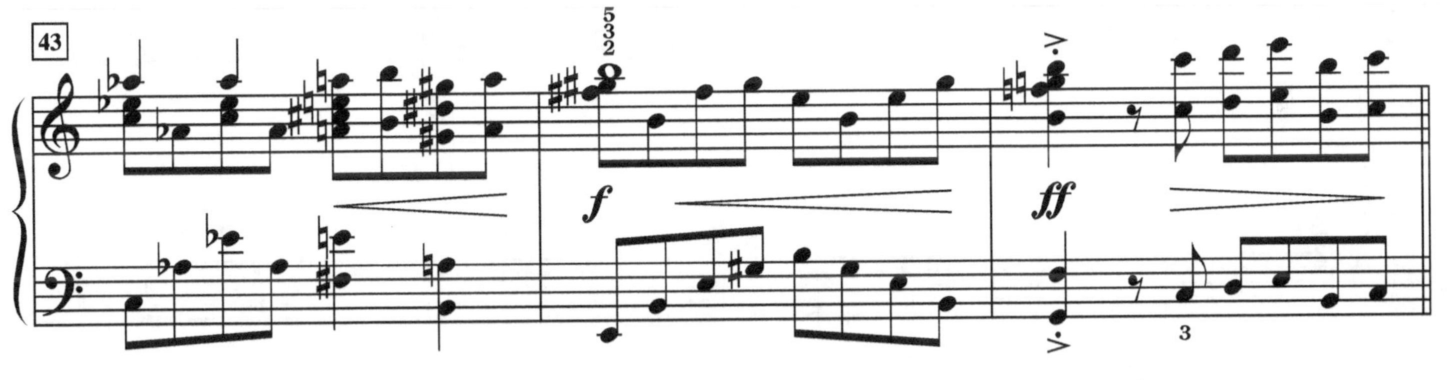

Broadway Hits

8va
49
52
55
ff
f
58
mf
dim.
61
8va
mp
p

Part of Your World
(from *The Little Mermaid*)

Music by Alan Menken
lyrics by Howard Ashman
Arranged by Dan Coates

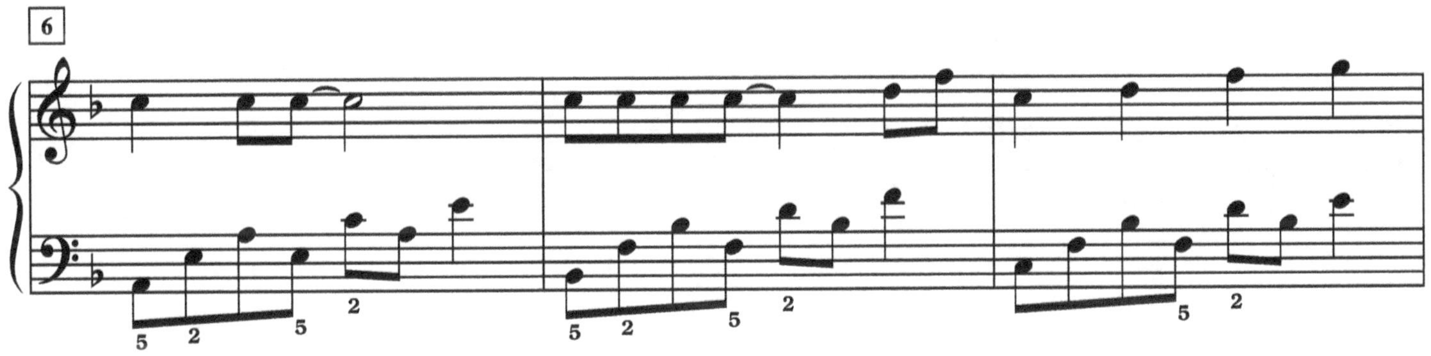

12

15

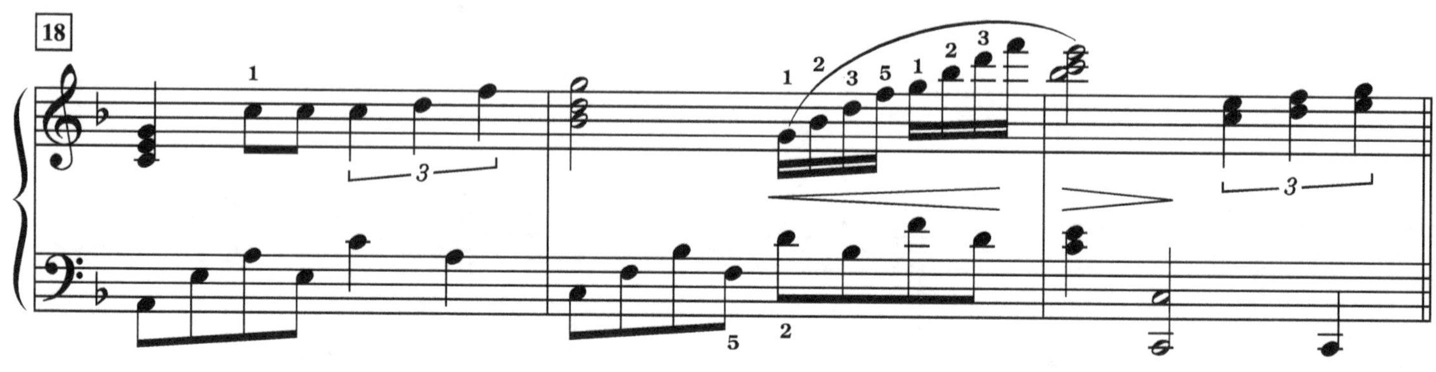
18

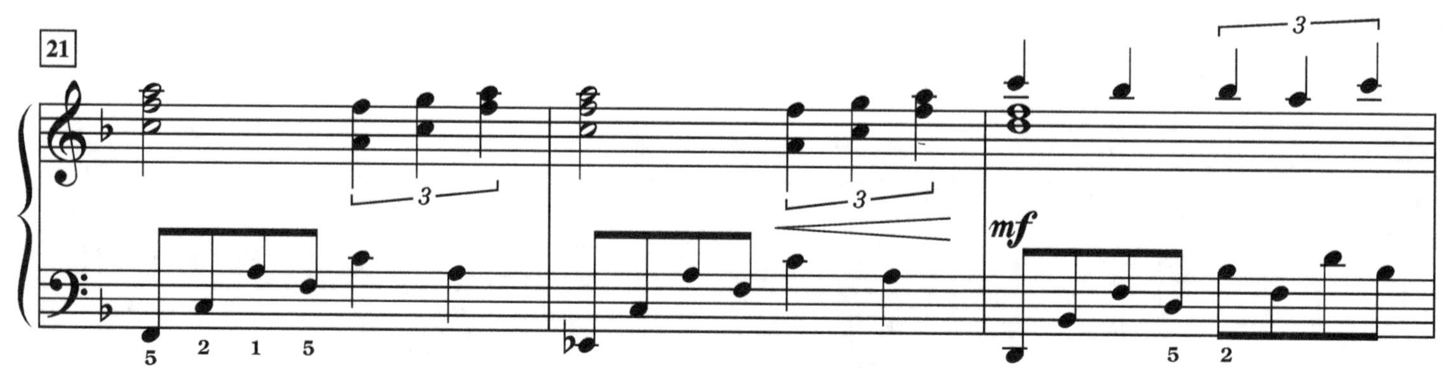
21
mf

24
27
mp
mf
30
4-5
33
36

39
42
dim.
45
mp
48
51
mf

54
57
mp
60
63
dim.
8va
66
p
rit.
pp

People
(from *Funny Girl*)

Words by Bob Merrill
Music by Jule Styne
Arranged by Dan Coates

11
espressivo

14
mf

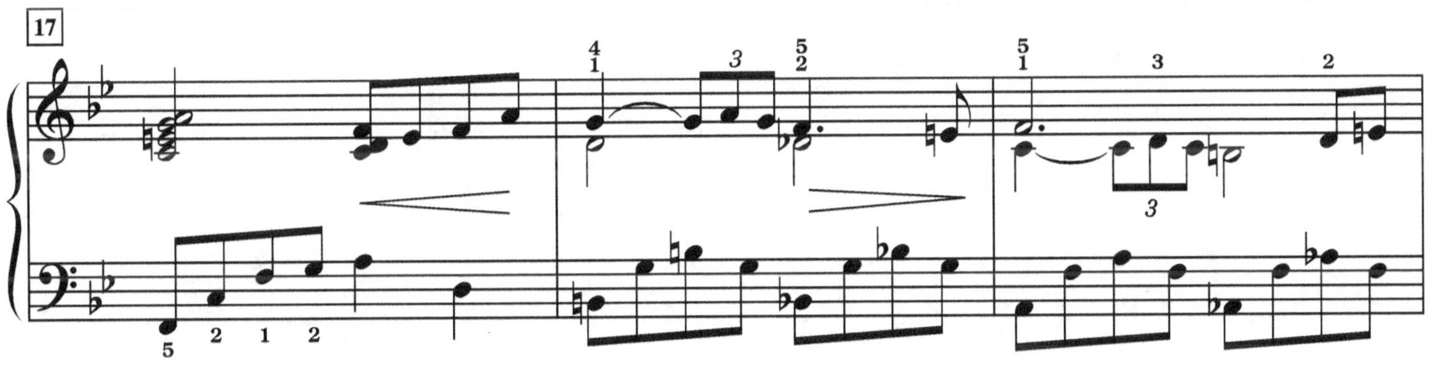
17

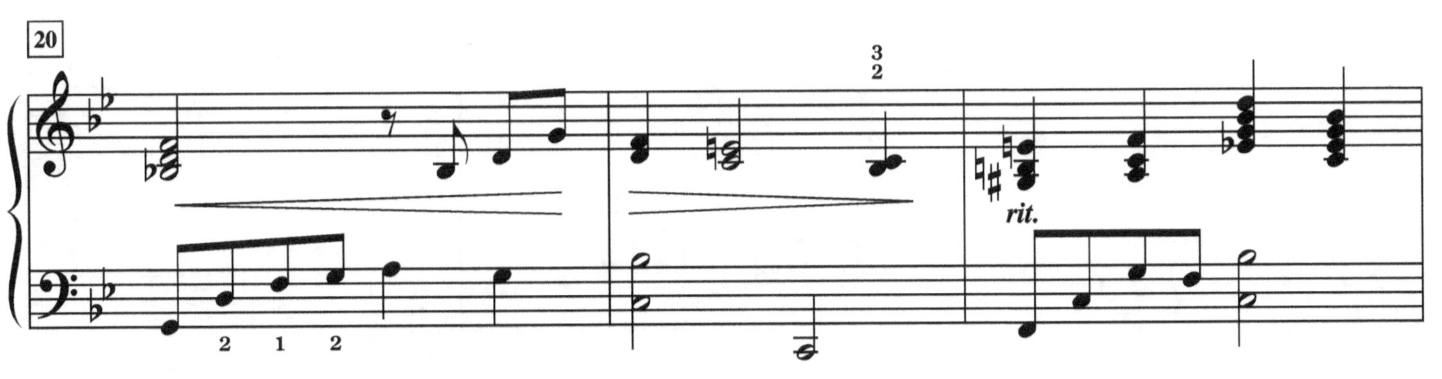
20
rit.

23
a tempo
mp

26
mf

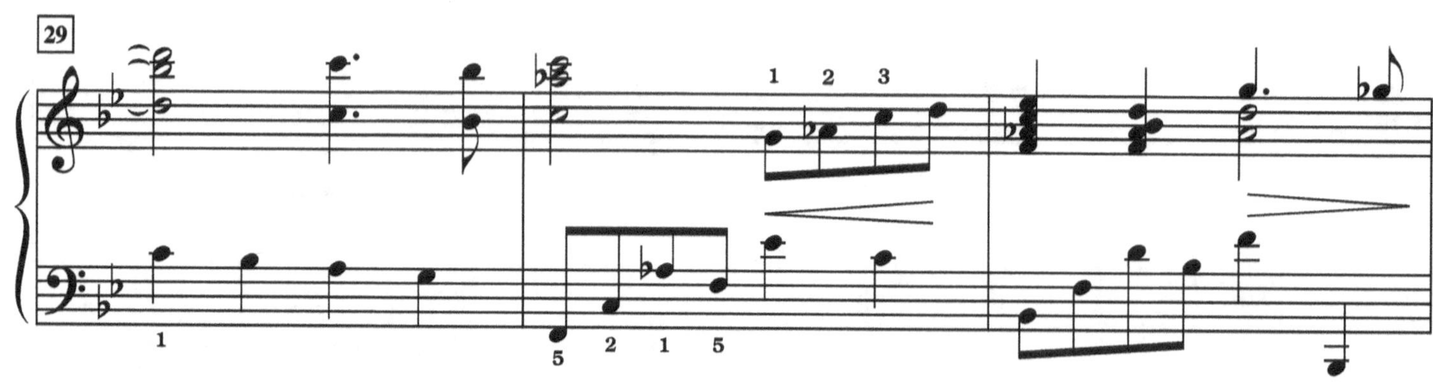
29

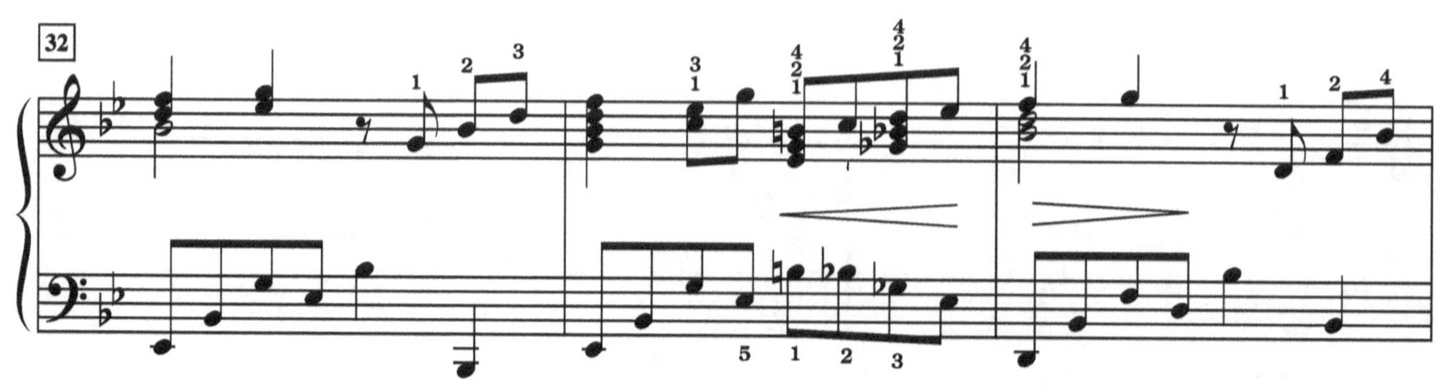
32

35
38
41
44
48
1.
2.
f
mf
ff
rit.
8va

Suddenly, Seymour
(from *Little Shop of Horrors*)

Words by Howard Ashman
Music by Alan Menken
Arranged by Dan Coates

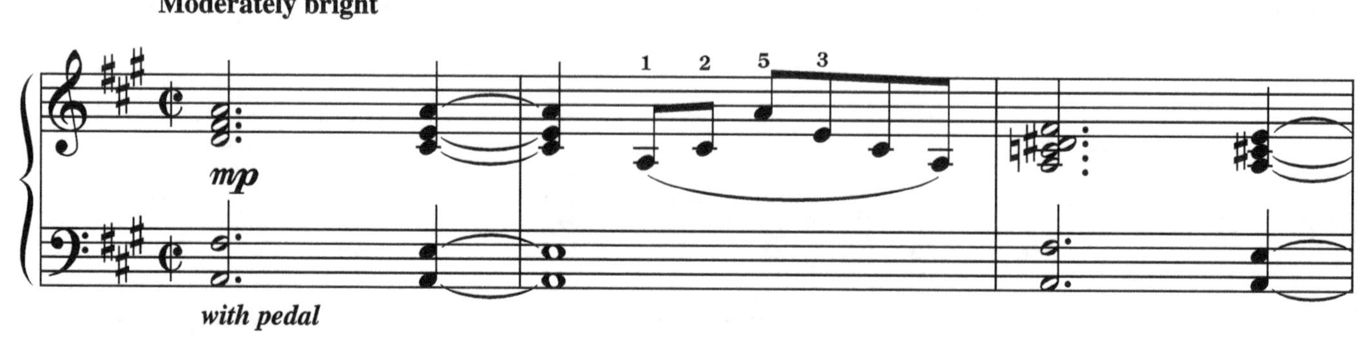

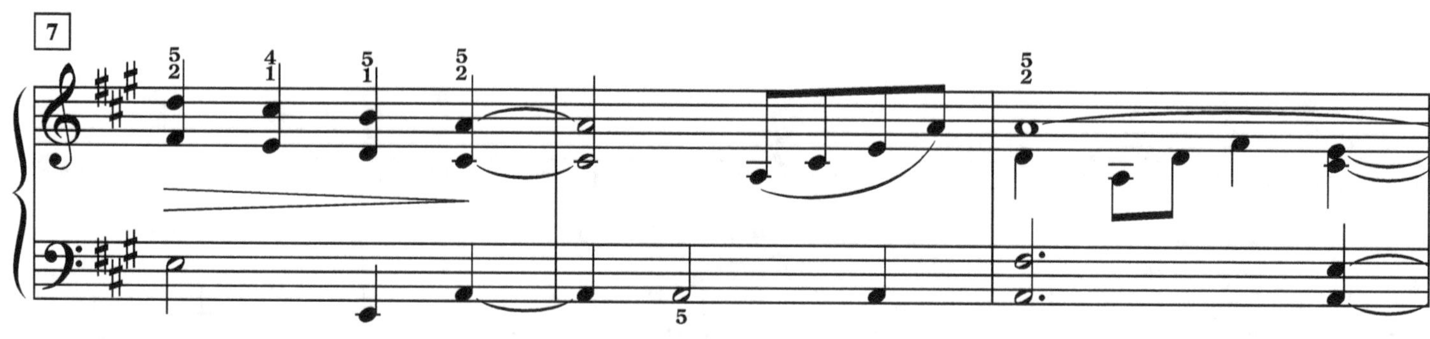

13
mp

16

19
mf

22

25
3
2
1
3

28
5
3 5
2 3 1 2 3
5 2 1 2
5–1

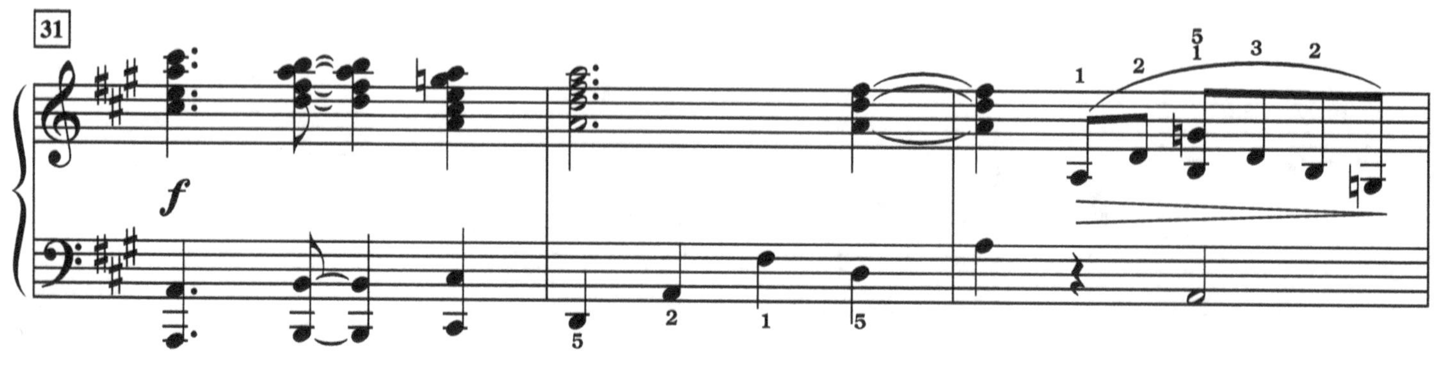
31
f
1 2
5
1
3 2
5 2 1 5

34
4
2
1
5

37
1

40
5

43
4
2
1
5
2
2

46
5
1
5
2
1
5

49
1
5
2

52
to Coda
2

55
ff
2

58
mf

61

64
D.S. al Coda

Coda
ff

71

74

77
ff
f

81

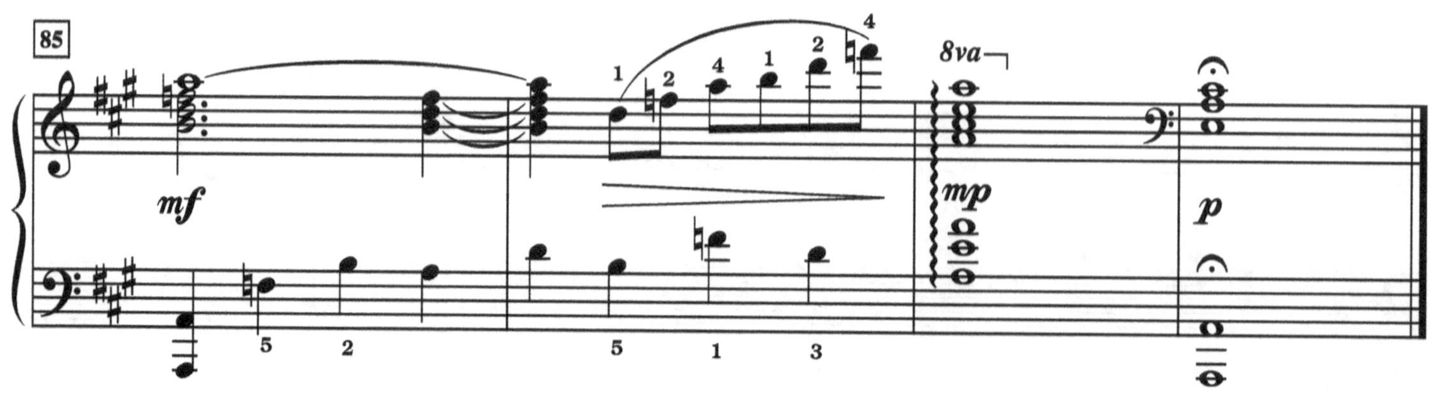
85
mf
8va
mp
p

Try to Remember
(from *The Fantasticks*)

Lyrics by Tom Jones
Music by Harvey Schmidt
Arranged by Dan Coates

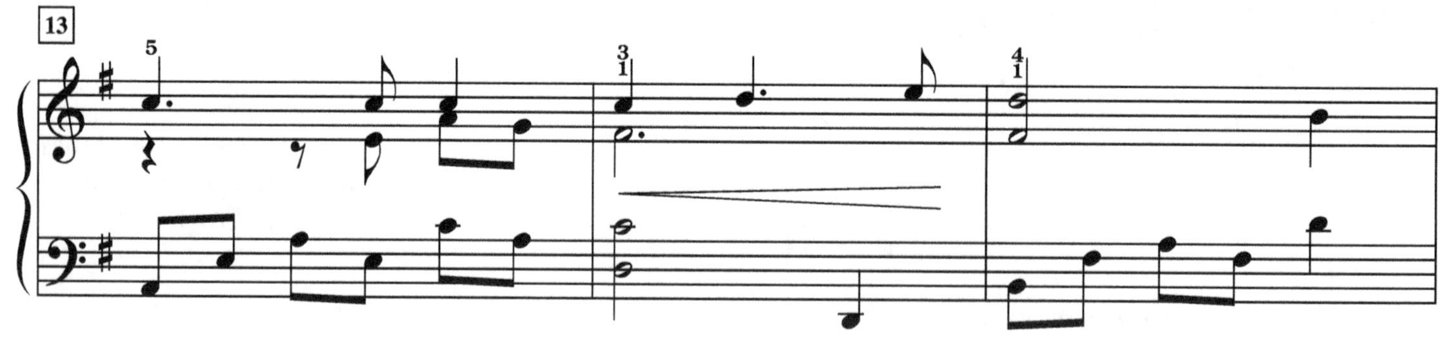
13
5
3
1
4
1

16
5
1
1
2
2
3
1
2
3

19
mf
3
2
3
2

22
3
5

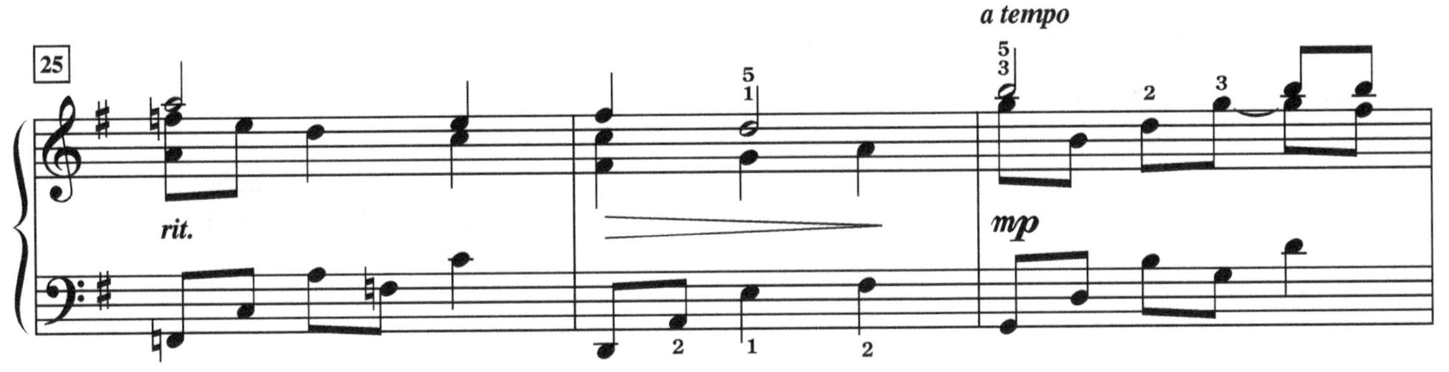
a tempo
25
rit.
mp

28

31
8va
mp
dim. poco a poco
rit.

34
p
molto rit.
pp

THE WINNER TAKES IT ALL
(FROM *MAMMA MIA!*)

Words and Music by
Benny Andersson and Bjorn Ulvaeus
Arranged by Dan Coates

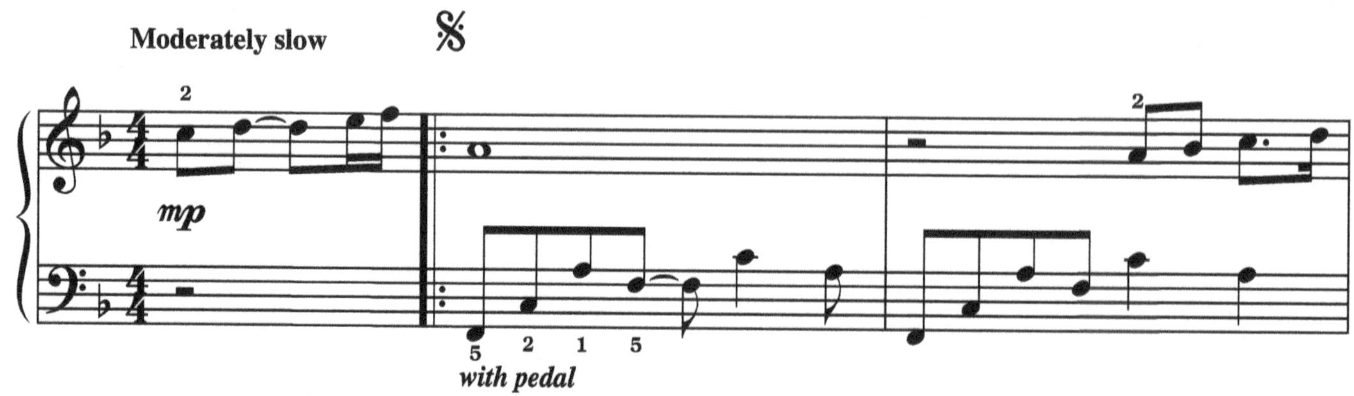

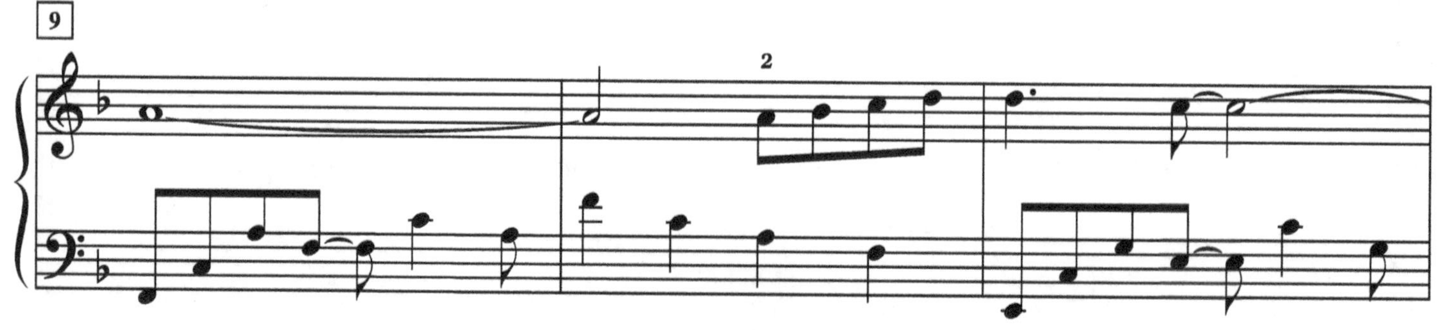

11

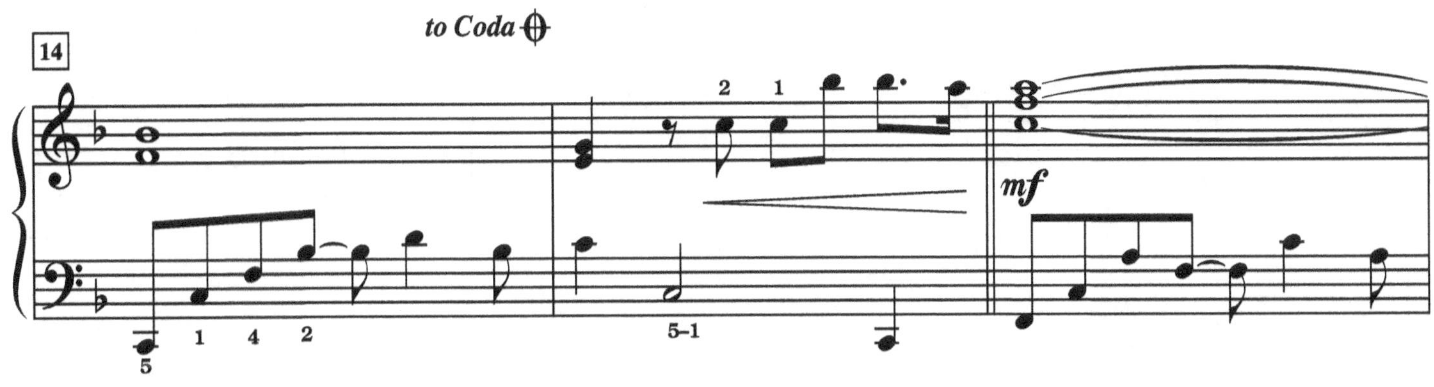
14
to Coda
mf

17

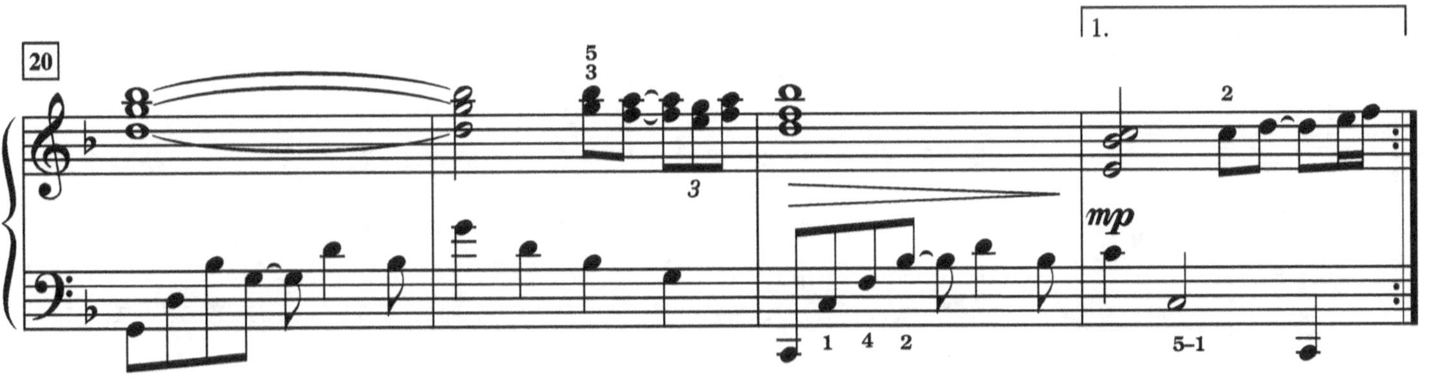
20
1.
mp

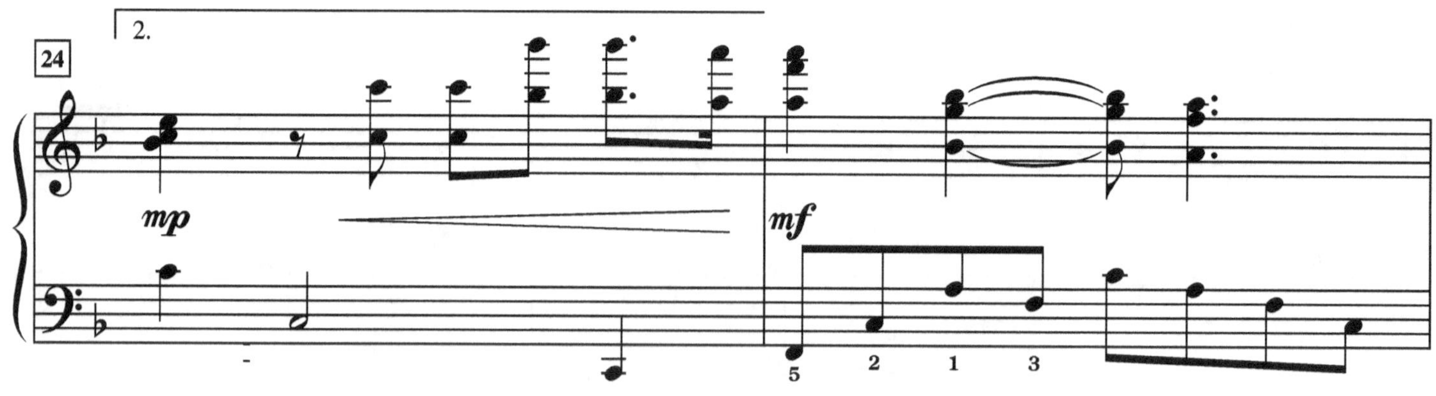

24
2.
mp
mf
5 2 1 3

26
8va
1
3

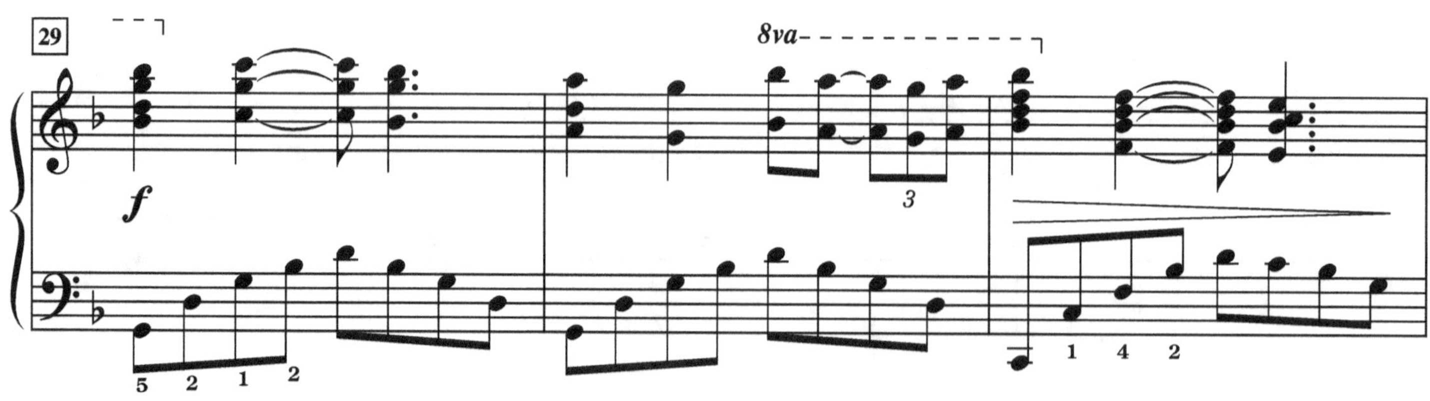

29
8va
f
3
5 2 1 2
1 4 2

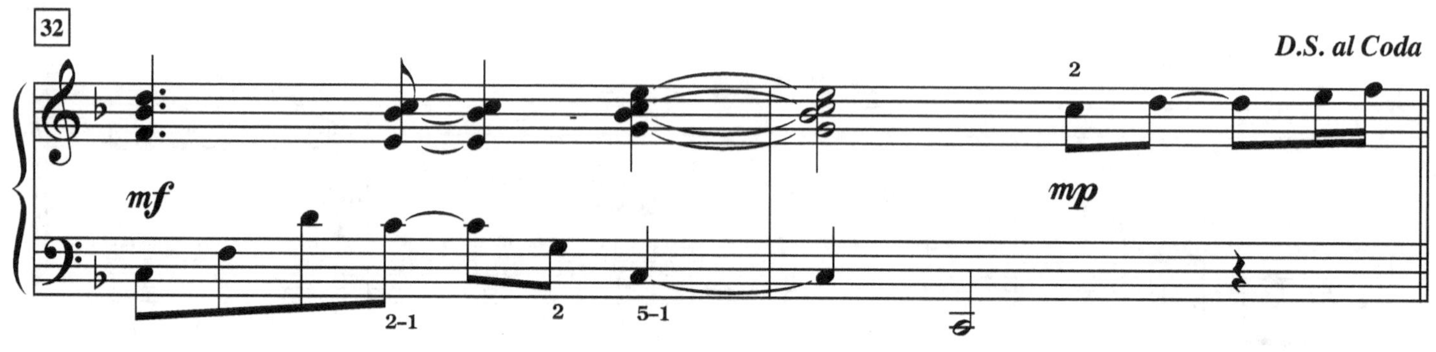

32
D.S. al Coda
mf
mp
2
2–1
2
5–1

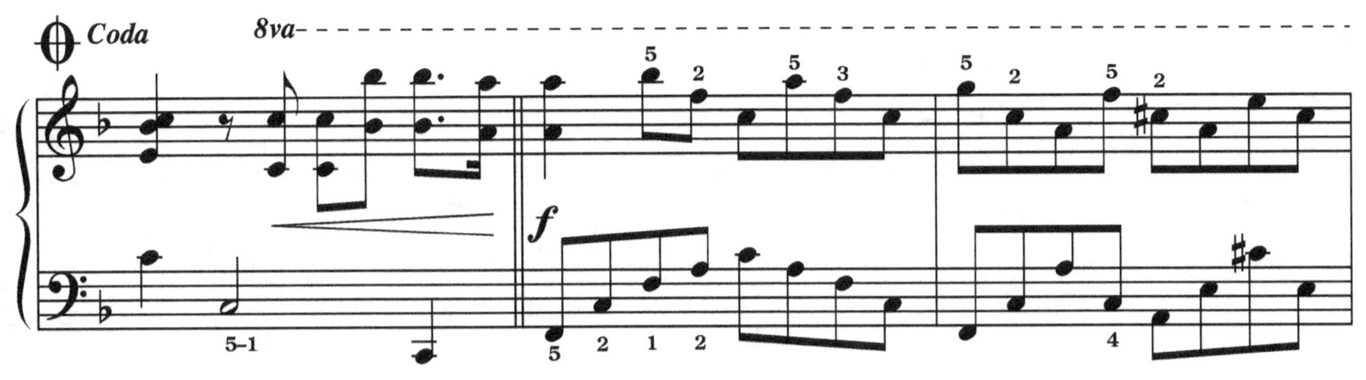
Coda
8va
f

37

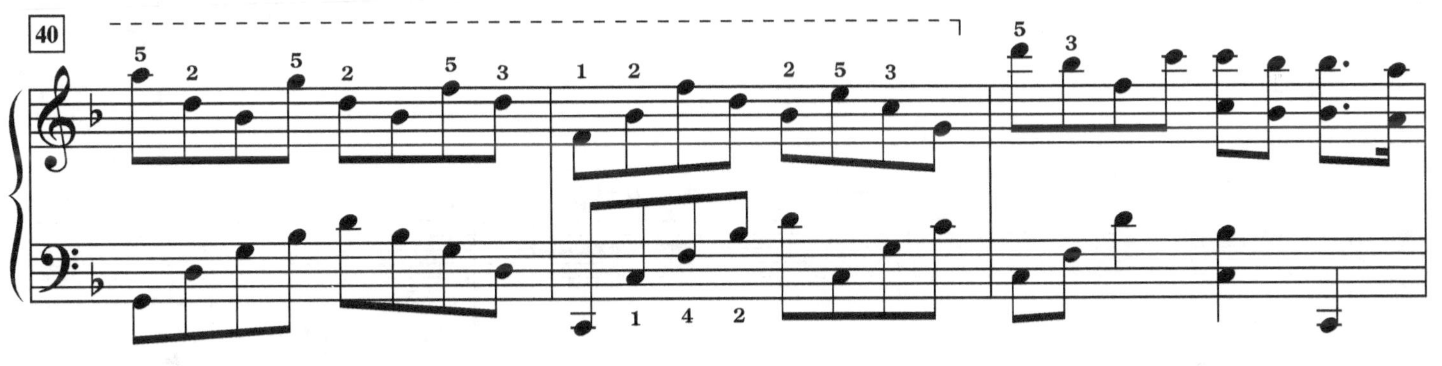
40

43

46
8va
1
49
dim.
2
mp
5
52
2
55
5
3
58
8va
2
1
4
p
1
2
rit.
pp
2